REFLECTIONS ON

Doing Your Great Work

IN ANY OCCUPATION

Books by Cheryl Lafferty Eckl

Non-Fiction: For Times of Dramatic Change

A Beautiful Death:
Keeping the Promise of Love

A Beautiful Grief:
Reflections on Letting Go

The LIGHT Process:
Living on the Razor's Edge of Change

Wise Inner Counselor Books
Reflections on Being Your True Self in Any Situation
Reflections on Doing Your Great Work in Any Occupation

Wise Inner Counselor Retreat
Thrive Through Chaos in Every Situation

Poetry: For Inspiration & Beauty

Poetics of Soul & Fire

Bridge to the Otherworld

Idylls from the Garden of Spiritual Delights & Healing

Sparks of Celtic Mystery:
soul poems from Éire

A Beautiful Joy: Reunion with the Beloved
Through Transfiguring Love

Fiction: For the Love of Twin Flames

The Weaving:
A Novel of Twin Flames Through Time

Twin Flames of Éire Trilogy
The Ancients and The Call
The Water and The Flame
The Mystics and The Mystery

A Wise Inner Counselor™ Book

REFLECTIONS ON

Doing Your Great Work

IN ANY OCCUPATION

Cheryl Lafferty Eckl

FLYING CRANE PRESS

REFLECTIONS ON DOING YOUR GREAT WORK IN ANY OCCUPATION
© 2021 Cheryl J. Eckl
A Wise Inner Counselor™ Book
Wise Inner Counselor™ | Soul Poetics™

Published by Flying Crane Press, Livingston, Montana 59047
Cheryl@CherylEckl.com | www.CherylEckl.com

Select images and art not the author's own are used by permission of the artist or photographer; or are free stock images from pexels.com, pixabay.com, pixy.org, stocksnap.io, unsplash.com; or from NASA.gov Ames Research Center; or are royalty-free purchases of standard permitted use images through 123rf.com, istock.com, bigstockphoto.com, stock.adobe.com.

Library of Congress Control Number: 2021904941
ISBN: 978-1-7367123-2-0 (paperback)
ISBN: 978-1-7367123-3-7 (e-book)

Printed in the United States of America

To all who would do
their great work

Dear Reader,

Reflections on Doing Your Great Work began over twenty years ago as a guide to excellence for executive assistants—a position I had held in a diverse, non-profit organization.

At different times, I was a high-level aide to multiple supervisors and department heads, the company's president and several members of the Board of Directors. Serving in these varied functions gave me a window into how work "works" that has been invaluable as my life and occupations have evolved.

While I enjoyed being good at my job, after several years I began to think about changing careers—although, in reality, I was afraid to actually make such a dramatic leap from the familiar into the unknown.

While I hesitated, my life abruptly changed anyway when I was seriously injured in a single-car accident. Now I was compelled to resign because I was no longer able to perform even simple tasks, let alone a complex job that demanded high efficiency.

This loss of my career was devastating. I was consumed with doubt, self-pity and even anger that my identity as a highly competent professional had been so suddenly stripped from me.

As a way of dealing with these troubling emotions, I began to write recollections of the meaningful work I had done in the past. Recording what I came to see as my legacy gave me a new lease on life. It also opened the door to the exciting new career path that eventually came my way as the creator and presenter of professional development workshops and training programs.

Then, in the midst of my growing success in this second career, another unexpected event turned my world upside down. My beloved husband was diagnosed with terminal cancer. This news shocked us to the core, but Stephen was determined that we both should keep working. So I continued to travel for my job as an instructor, and he soldiered on for four more years.

Eventually, he did ask me to stay home because his need for

my support was increasing—especially on weekends. On weekdays he was still pushing himself to retain some semblance of normalcy by going to work. But by now the effort was exhausting.

To stay emotionally grounded and keep myself busy while Stephen fulfilled his desire to work as long as possible, I focused on completing a series of chapters on the insights I had gained in pursuit of that mysterious quality we call "great work."

I put the finishing touches on a first draft of a book less than three months before Stephen died—and then did not pick it up again for nearly a decade.

As it turned out, my thoughts and feelings about effective behaviors and attitudes in work and life needed time to mature and to percolate through the cycles of dramatic growth and changing perspectives that have unfolded in my world since Stephen's death.

The most significant aspect of that process has been my increased understanding of how the presence of the inner voice, which I call the Wise Inner Counselor™ or True Self, has been the deciding factor for me in my professional and personal development.

So, the book that began as a treatise on how to make work meaningful and fulfilling is now two books—*Doing Your Great Work in Any Occupation* and *Being Your True Self in Any Situation*.

Each volume is a collection of reflections on basic principles that allow all of our endeavors to flow from the heart of wise inner guidance. I hope these thoughts will be useful to the great work that only you can do and to the enhancement of who you are being in the process.

May your Wise Inner Counselor guide and guard you all the days of your life.

Cheryl Lafferty Eckl
Spring 2021

CONTENTS

*To achieve your soul's
limitless potential,
follow the voice
of your True Self.*

*Therein lies the road
to great work.*

—The Wise Inner Counselor™

PART ONE

Reflecting on Great Work

Reflection 1

GREAT WORK AS A DESTINATION ONLY YOU CAN DISCOVER

What does great work look like? How does it feel to do great work? These are the questions I set out to answer.

A Passion for Work

I am passionate about work—not work as drudgery or mindless toil, but as the highest expression of who we are. As that special purpose for which we were born. As the opportunity to do and be our best. To share the noblest part of ourselves—the part that is true and caring, honest, trustworthy and responsible.

It is how and why we work that fascinates me. Work is where we make or break ourselves. Where we prove what we are made of. Where we strive to make something of our efforts that has deep and lasting meaning. And, ideally, where we leave the world a little better than we found it.

The World Needs Our Gifts and Talents

Like it or not, the world of work is changing and it is desperate for our contribution. We may have to search for opportunities, but they do exist for us to discover and create our best work ever.

Probably because my early training was in theater, I have never followed a traditional career path. I have had to ferret out next steps without much outer guidance. Discovering those steps has been quite an adventure, and I am still surprised by what shows up when I find myself ready for a change. And, then, of course, sometimes change happens before I am quite ready.

When the Territory Changes

Several years ago I moved back to Denver after an eighteen-year absence. I brought with me an old map on which I lovingly traced the routes I had traveled to school and a variety of jobs. I was excited to be returning to the land of my youth.

But the territory had changed. The dirt lane leading to the dinner theater where I had performed was now paved with its own highway exit.

Old South Broadway Boulevard no longer dead-ended at a hilly country road that skirted the edge of a vast ranch. Multiple sub-divisions now covered the land where cattle had grazed. New South Broadway extended all the way through these developments to a six-lane freeway that looped the city.

Denver had experienced more dramatic growth than I could have imagined. The hometown that I thought I knew so well was now foreign to me. I needed a new map.

We Often Do Not See the Old Maps

In moving back to my hometown, the need for an updated map was obvious. Such is not always the case in our work life.

Although we may acknowledge the necessity of charting a new course, we may be so accustomed to the old maps that we remain unaware of being short-changed by outdated assumptions.

We are like the proverbial goldfish that is oblivious to the water in which it swims. We are comfortable in our fishbowl. But there is a big ocean out there, just waiting for us to dive in—if we are willing to risk the waves of change.

Intellectually, we know that established maps of inner and outer landscapes are only as good as the latest discovery. However, in our search for stability in an unpredictable world, we tend to latch onto the familiar as if it were permanent in hopes of staving off the turbulence we sense all around us. Much to our detriment.

Maps That Limit Us

Organizational charts and job descriptions may offer little insight into the actual tasks that people are performing daily in offices, assembly lines, call centers and construction sites around the world.

Salary structures hardly represent the value an individual brings to his or her occupation. Emojis, texts and social media posts do not begin to tap the creative possibilities of human communication. Popular culture's formulaic representation of romantic love is a far cry from the wellspring of the human heart.

The SAT exam measures only mathematical and linguistic skills—merely a slice of the boundless territory of multiple human intelligences.[1]

Many self-identification tools fall short of defining the complex individuals we are. Even the most effective psychological modalities represent only a fraction of the human psyche's depth.

An Early Map of Great Work

For several years my work involved considerable travel where I met exceptional leaders, janitors, farmers, artists, musicians, security guards, waitstaff, managers, builders, entrepreneurs, baristas and others—all doing their jobs with focus, intention, commitment and a smile.

I was intrigued to meet these people because they each brought an extra spark to their occupations. They understood that work is more than what you do. It is how you are being in the process. And in that process, they transformed their efforts from mere activity to elegant artistry—from "just a job" to a labor of love.

I called these inspiring individuals "Total Professionals" and even named my first business TotalPros. I soon began writing about people who wanted to be completely professional in whatever work they were called to by circumstance or personal preference.

I found myself asking: What do these Total Professionals do differently from their colleagues and co-workers?

And in that same vein, what are the behaviors and attitudes of great customers? If you could describe the perfect client, what characteristics would you include?

Eventually, I created a map based on the twelve letters of the word "professional." [2] For me, this concept of how great work is both created and received by anybody anywhere became a tool that helped me evaluate the quality of my own endeavors and that proved useful when I started developing my own workshops.

The Map Is Not the Territory
Of course, every explorer knows that to understand the landscape, you have to get out and walk. Build up a good sweat and a few blisters. Get your boots dirty. Enjoy the process.

Keep a well-tested map in your back pocket, but do not be afraid to stray off the beaten path. Treasures of discovery await those who venture out into the uncharted territory of a life well lived and work done greatly.

For the next twenty years, that is exactly what I did. I dug into work and life and tested my map. I observed people doing great work in the several organizations where I was employed. I talked to students who attended my professional development courses about what it meant to excel in their industries.

We Need a Guide, Not a Map
While the exterior landscape of work continues to change with breathtaking speed, the fundamental principles, behaviors and attitudes that I identified in the Total Professionals still apply.

Perhaps now more than ever, these transferable skills are essential for doing great work in any occupation. However, as old industries disappear and new ones appear, we need more than a time-tested map in our back pocket.

Everybody and everything is in motion. So how do we navigate this wild world of work if no part of life stands still long enough to be mapped? What we need is an internal guidance system that allows us to operate like a human gyroscope—spinning rapidly around the axis of self that is free to change direction, however circumstances require.

Inner Wisdom to the Rescue

Fortunately, we already have such a guide. Unfortunately, we have not been told that going where this wise inner voice leads is the secret to traversing the rugged landscape of today's multidimensional, multicultural, multigenerational world of work and life.

Nearly every conceptual system has a name for this voice: intuition, conscience, inner wisdom. I call it the True Self or the Wise Inner Counselor.

You may have encountered this inner guide in times of crisis. Or perhaps a sense of "just knowing" has shown up as inspiration for a new idea or an innovative way of expressing an old one.

Inner wisdom may have warned you against a decision that would have led to unanticipated negative consequences—especially if proponents of old maps were pushing you to do what you have always done.

Regardless of your occupation, heeding the Wise Inner Counselor is the best way I know for creating a life of meaning and work that makes a difference to families, companies, communities and nations.

The Journey of Great Doing

To become a doer of great work in the twenty-first century is to embark upon a journey aimed at exploring the vast richness that all our endeavors can offer us when we attune to inner guidance.

It is not a quick or easy trip. The mountain is always higher in the climbing than it appears at the start. Yet, as a wise mentor once told me, the upward trek is worth the inconvenience.

My hope is that these reflections will inspire you to greater depth of self-awareness and improved relationships with others. And while you enhance your skills, knowledge and competencies, may you also discover more sincere appreciation for your personal values, beliefs, thoughts, goals and aspirations.

Transcending the Old Maps

Great work carves a path through life that circles back to first principles again and again. Therefore, my purpose is to encourage you to examine your work and your life—what you do, how you do it, what you want from it and how you can transcend the old maps that prevent you from exceeding your own expectations.

Doing Your Great Work points to a destination only you can discover and whose summit only you can achieve. As you make that journey, may you accomplish truly great work in a life well lived. Your efforts will surely make the world a better place—especially when you engage your inner wisdom, the X factor of all great work.

Reflection 2

INNER WISDOM: THE X FACTOR OF DOING GREAT WORK

*You have a built-in superpower. How will
you use it to do and be your best?*

Observing What Was Missing

When I began teaching management courses, I quickly realized that
many of the issues which attendees brought to class were matters of
how people were being rather than what they were doing.

All too often, the behaviors or performance problems they
hoped to correct through training emerged from limited or limiting attitudes about themselves and their co-workers. Or about how
they did or did not fit together.

As an instructor, my job was to teach the course material. Yet
I could see that what was missing for many of these fine people was
conscious and consistent engagement with their own inner wisdom.

Fortunately, the courses I taught gave me some opportunity
to help them shift their attention toward their innate talents and
away from so much reliance on external factors. But what I really
wanted to emphasize was the fact that they already had within them
the best manager they could ever want.

Removers of Obstacles

The really superb managers I have worked for have been masters of facilitating great work by removing the obstacles that prevented people from doing their best.

These managers protected their employees from unreasonable rules and regulations, cumbersome processes and interfering administrations. Their mantra was: "Tell me how I can help."

The Wise Inner Counselor goes them one better. Its consistent message is: "Pay attention. I know how to help you." I have found this to be true both on and off the job.

In the corporate classroom, I learned to trust what my intuition was telling me to do or say to bring home a point or to spark deeper engagement from the class.

If I heard something, I said something. My students were often amazed when I articulated what they were thinking or answered a question before they asked it. When I followed inner guidance, my instructor evaluations were always excellent.

These experiences and countless others have convinced me that heeding our Wise Inner Counselor's direction can make all the difference in both our professional and personal lives.

Paying Attention to Valid Warnings

Inner wisdom can warn us in many ways. Sometimes we get a gut feeling that a certain person or situation is not safe. At other times an image of impending calamity will come to mind. Or we "just know" that something is amiss.

Of course, the alert is only as effective as the attention you pay to it. This was brought home to me in a conversation with a crisis management team that was researching how distractions and assumptions can block vital warnings on which lives depend.

They told the story of Eastern Airlines Flight 401 that crashed in 1972. The disaster could have been avoided if the pilot and his co-pilot had obeyed the warning chime signaling loss of altitude that was too gradual to be detected by the crew as they flew over the Atlantic Ocean on a moonless night.

Instead, they were distracted by a malfunctioning landing gear light. They did not hear the chime and remained under the false impression that they had plenty of altitude until the plane crashed in the Florida Everglades resulting in 101 fatalities.

Just-in-Time Prompting Saves Lives

Our internal early-warning system can indeed save lives—such as the time a friend of mine was suddenly prompted to step back from the path of an earth mover on a construction site just before the machine would have mashed him into the ground.

When we cram every waking minute with activity, we rob ourselves of the opportunity to sense the rich, creative solutions or intuitive promptings that can arise from quieting our minds.

It is no mistake that many of us get our best ideas while walking, driving, taking a shower or cleaning house. In those moments of mental spaciousness, the Wise Inner Counselor may rescue us.

"I Have to Leave Right Now!"

Saturday, August 15, 1997 was a bright, clear day in Corwin Springs, Montana. My husband was flying home that evening after a week's conference in Washington, D. C. I planned to pick him up at the airport in Bozeman. Then we would enjoy a late dinner and spend the night in town to do some shopping the following day.

Around 4:30 p.m. I was cleaning our apartment when I heard myself declare in response to a very powerful inner prompting, "I have to leave right now!"

Over the years, I had learned to pay attention to those urgent messages. So I threw my overnight bag in the car and took off north on Highway 89—a two-lane ribbon of asphalt that runs through the narrows of Yankee Jim Canyon, opening out into the broad expanse of Paradise Valley as it follows the Yellowstone River along the majestic Absaroka Mountains.

Just past the canyon I became distracted and wandered too far to the right. I swerved to miss a mile marker, over-corrected, lost control of my car and ended up driving along a ditch at 60 miles an hour—only to hit a driveway incline that launched my car into an adjoining field where it landed flat.

Why Did the Accident Happen?

People have asked me, "If your Wise Inner Counselor is so great, why did the accident happen?"

To me, this was the mercy of what could be called a "karmic mitigation." We come into this life with obligations from past lives that must be made right. That is the cosmic law of "what goes around comes around." Burdens that we have placed upon life through words and deeds must be balanced by our positive actions—and sometimes by experiencing difficult circumstances or accidents.

My sense of this event is that my going through it was the most effective way for me to pay a certain karmic debt from the past.

The circumstances of the accident were a miracle of what did not happen. My car did not roll. There was no opposing traffic—which could have included huge trucks, elk or the Big Horn Sheep for whom this is a migration corridor. There was still plenty of daylight, so some motorists saw the accident and stopped to help me.

Although I was seriously injured, I lived to tell the tale. All because I had long ago learned to trust those inner promptings to see me safely to where I needed to be—just in time.

Inner Wisdom as the X Factor

How do top performers decide what action to take in any situation? Excellent training is an important foundation. Experience counts. Just ask insurance adjusters about the higher risk involved with inexperienced drivers.

Yet great work resonates with an ineffable "something" that

can elevate even the most mundane of tasks. Not everybody will admit to acting based on inner wisdom. But some of my more courageous students have told me things like: "I just knew what to do." "The solution came to me in the middle of the night."

Insight. Inner knowing. Flashes of illumination. A complete concept that comes sailing into your awareness almost like a golden orb. Each one is a manifestation of the Wise Inner Counselor in action, and you have that brilliance right at your fingertips.

As you pursue your own great work, I encourage you to maintain a listening ear, an open mind and a willing heart. Trust your early warning system and take action when the voice of inner wisdom speaks. I predict that the more you pay attention, the more your work and life will improve.

Reflection 3

FINDING GREAT WORK
IN ANY OCCUPATION

A good paycheck alone does not constitute a great job.
The people I know want something more meaningful.

What Do We Want from Work?

I believe we want from work what we want from life: purpose, respect, dignity, fairness, opportunity for growth.

I recently asked a young man what he was looking for in a job. He had been laid off from an industry that is experiencing radical change, so the question was apropos his current situation. Here is what he said:

> I've been asked this exact question in a couple of job interviews. Coming from retail, I'm looking for a job where I can sit in a chair, not work nights, weekends or holidays, and hopefully get paid enough to afford living on my own. This isn't what I tell the hiring managers, though.
>
> More seriously, I am looking for a job where I can be proud of the work I do—something more meaningful than selling merchandise or convincing people to sign up for credit cards.

Also, since I'm still relatively new to the job market, I'd like a position that will allow me to learn new skills that look good on a resume (maybe a new software program or just something more desirable than how to perfect a display).

Obviously, I'd like a nice office environment and a company that isn't at risk of going out of business. In a way, this lay-off was good for me as now I get the chance to do something new that's more relevant for where I want to go with my career trajectory.

I suspect most of us have expressed the same desires. I have definitely been in this fellow's shoes. He admitted to being bitter toward the industry he just left—which I understand.

And yet, over the years I have learned that every job is a stepping stone to what comes next. Former employment experiences have never been wasted—even those miserable times of getting fired. Here is what I shared with this bright young man:

Lay-offs and firings can be tough. They also can be a good thing—perhaps life's rather shocking way of telling us it's time to move on to the next phase that will bring us closer to who we really are.

Keep being real each day, and life will bring your next step. Identifying the factors you list is very useful. I once realized that I needed light yellow walls to really thrive in an office, and I got them.

Bitterness will only rob you of the energy you need to be in tune with what's next. You have too many talents to waste your time looking back. Trust me.

Be grateful and look ahead. This is only a blip, even though it feels like a chasm right now. The test is how you respond because that is what you can control.

My friend did eventually find a good job which included many of the preferences he listed. He is now well on his way to doing work that can make a difference to himself and others.

More Ideas About What We Want from Work

When I asked some of my instructor colleagues and students from my professional development classes what they wanted from their occupations, they offered these ideas:

- We want to be accountable for outcomes that stretch us, while using our unique talents and creativity to accomplish them.

- We want to be mentored by people with experience greater than our own in an atmosphere of dynamic interaction and mutual respect.

- We want to be fairly compensated for our efforts, rewarded for extraordinary contributions and valued for who we are—not only for what we do.

- We are drawn to work that matches our talents. And we want to talk about it, share it and improve it within a community of equally motivated individuals.

- We want the freedom to do our best and to extend that freedom to others. We view anything less as tyranny.

- We expect everyone to carry his or her weight and to abide by an unwritten contract that says we will be treated generously by those we report to, while we do the same for those whom we supervise.

To Make a Difference, Bloom Where You're Planted

This is a lot to expect, and we are often disappointed. But we keep striving and sometimes we actually do find our dream job. In that case, the challenge becomes: How do we keep it fresh, dynamic, interesting and creative? Or suppose we have a decent position that, while not our ultimate goal, is the best opportunity at present? How do we make the most of it?

For years I kept a poster on my office wall that proclaimed: "Bloom where you're planted!" How do we do that?

When we understand how work "works," I am convinced we will achieve better on-the-job results with more personal satisfaction and fulfillment.

When we understand that competencies are only part of the story of effective work, and when we consistently follow the promptings of inner guidance, I am certain that we will dig beneath the surface of job descriptions and titles to the essence of what makes work great. And, more to the point, what can make anyone great at work.

Bloom Where You're Planted!

Reflection 4

WHAT DOES IT MEAN
TO BE GREAT?

*There are hundreds of definitions for "greatness." How we
define it depends on circumstances, perspectives and context.*

Many Situations, Many Meanings

We say "great minds" and laugh when we and another person come
up with the same idea at the same time.

When we call someone "great," we often mean that they
have a generous heart, a magnanimous attitude toward others, a
demeanor that is kind with an orientation toward service—usually
for causes that resonate with our own core values.

"Great" often defines results and the ability to produce them.
A great business plan anticipates significant financial gain. A great
athlete excels in near-impossible feats of strength and agility. Great
leaders accomplish goals that improve the lives of everyone.

Finding Another Gear

I once read a quote about exceptional performance saying that "the
great ones just find another gear." Although that statement was
made about an outstanding racehorse, I think we can learn a lesson
from the concept.

A big part of being great is finding that extra gear. For humans, I believe that gear is inner wisdom, which we can apply to even mundane tasks that may never make us famous.

For me and my closest colleagues, the key to doing great work has always been to fully commit to the tasks before us while paying close attention to what our Wise Inner Counselor is trying to get through to us.

Although we may never attain renown outside of our families, places of work or communities, when we engage our inner wisdom and resist the creeping societal mediocrity that homogenizes its members to the lowest common denominator, greatness is at hand.

Striving for the Boundless

We may experience a profound exhilaration when witnessing extraordinary deeds performed by individuals or groups that tap into their talents with fortitude and perseverance.

One of the reasons I have always loved live theater, music and dance is the opportunity to witness an inspired production that elevates the audience and the performers themselves to a sublime shared experience.

In these moments of exceptional human accomplishment we may encounter what renowned poet Henry Wadsworth Longfellow called "the boundless reach of sky."

Who Are We Being in the Doing?

The longer I have spent exploring the concept of great work, the more clearly have I come to realize that we cannot separate who we are being from what we are doing. Throughout history, truly great individuals, groups, movements and nations have apparently known this to be true.

Although we may try to leave personal issues at home, when we show up for work, we bring a complex being to the scene. Then the essential question becomes: Who are we being and what will our presence in any situation contribute to the positive outcomes that we and our co-workers hope to achieve?

In Search of Positive Greatness

When we study the lives of those who have been called great, we can learn a lot about who and what deserves the appellation.

At their best, great beings among us convey an uncommon nobility infused with gracious humility. In their presence, we may transcend the mundane. We may even share with them a touch of that boundless reach of sky.

Considering illustrious individuals from the past can be tricky, though, because we cannot help but view them through the perspective of current values and societal trends.

However, if we observe their lives through the lens of core values such as truth, beauty and goodness, we are likely to find some excellent examples. And we also encounter a problem. As soon as we start examining anyone's life in detail, we quickly discover that they were not perfect.

Do we then dismiss them as candidates for greatness? Or do we look deeper into other qualities that transcend an individual's inevitable humanness? Specifically, do we consider how they overcame their personal imperfections?

Expanding Our Definition

After twenty years of pondering what makes work great, I have come to the conclusion that greatness is too broad a term, perhaps too personal in our estimation, to be concretely defined.

I think we are better served by approaching it indirectly through observation and by meditation on how we are affected by the words, deeds and presence of someone who might be thought great.

As this book unfolds, I invite you to expand your definition of what your own great work might look like. Based on my reflections, here are some questions we can keep in mind.

I encourage you to develop your own thoughts. I am certain that for any of us, connecting with our own inner guidance to reveal the answers to these questions is the work of a lifetime.

Some Questions for Reflection

When we would be great, we do well to ask:

- Are we leaving the world a better place for our having been part of it?

- Are we lifting up others by looking out for their well-being and by offering them their own opportunities to be great?

- Do we tell the truth and promote truth-telling in others?

- Does our presence enhance the situations in which we are involved, making them seem lighter, more meaningful?

- Are we fearless in the face of obstacles to our best work?

- Do we consistently act in accordance with our core values, particularly when we are challenged by people or circumstances to compromise our principles?

- Do we aim for the highest good for all and build for the future?

- Do we acknowledge extraordinary individuals who have come before us and on whose shoulders we stand?

- Are we connected to something greater than ourselves?

Reflection 5

A Deeper Look at Great Work

*When we take time to look closely, our occupations
may reveal hidden depths. Great work always
shows us more about life and how to live it well.*

Great Work Is Efficient

When my husband, Stephen, was hired by the budget office at a major metropolitan school district, he was excited about the job. The hours were reasonable, and the benefits generous. It seemed the perfect fit—that is, until budget "crunch time" rolled around.

Stephen quickly discovered that the department head's approach to this daunting annual project was "work harder and longer." This was not my husband's way of doing anything. He was a systems thinker—always on the lookout for creative solutions to streamline processes. And he had a talent for it.

The challenge was that innovation demands change, and his supervisor had been using the same non-systematic methods for almost thirty years. She was nearing retirement and had no intention of altering her style.

So, in his own quiet manner, Stephen simplified his part of the budgeting process, got his work done and went home on time.

He also applied for a transfer to a department that would

appreciate his expertise and not demand that his employment interfere with the quality of his personal life.

Here is Stephen's philosophy for working efficiently:

- Work as hard as necessary to get the job done really well.
- Relish your accomplishments.
- End each day feeling well-spent.
- Stand up for great work that supports the goal of creating a life that is meaningful, fulfilling and joyful.

Obligations and Callings in Work and Life

As was brought home to me in the car accident that I survived, we are born into this life with obligations from past lives that we are meant to balance in this one. We also come into embodiment with the positive karma we have accrued for our past good works.

Understanding that our obligations often have to do with other people has helped me understand why some employment situations have been really difficult whereas others have been very pleasant.

Another aspect of work, which I happen to relish, is when our endeavors are less like an obligation and more like a calling.

Sometimes it is hard to tell the difference until a project has been completed, although what I have seen in my own life is that once a karmic obligation is fulfilled, that job goes away. Conversely, the opportunity to go deeper and deeper into a calling grows and gains greater meaning over time.

A Word About Commissions

Have you ever been engaged in a project that had a deeper significance to you than a simple job assignment? Did it have a tangible "felt sense" of being inspired by something greater than yourself? Did you approach it with more care or respect than other tasks?

That is the nature of a commission.

A commission can convey the sense that we are fulfilling a promise or a vow, perhaps even a sacred obligation that flows from the positive karma we have made in past lives. I have had people tell me about such experiences, and I have had them myself.

A commission can be subtle in the way it pervades every aspect of your life while you are working on it. It also can be amazingly powerful in the way it transcends all desires less than its own fulfillment.

From this perspective, a commission is a real labor of love—a truly worthy activity that enhances those who are doing it as well as those on whose behalf the commission is performed.

Great Work Is Joyful Work

There is a quality that shines out from great work which moves us when we witness it.

Think about watching a fantastic performance by an artist or athlete. A tender exchange between a parent and child. Heroic actions by first responders. Or the quiet steadiness of a power plant operator who keeps the lights on for an entire community during a time of crisis.

Great work touches the hearts of those who create it as well as those who receive it. A job well done inspires a particular kind of joy that often includes the desire to benefit others. And it is the grateful reception by customers, clients, audiences and families that completes the circle of accomplishment.

Great work reflects the True Self of the person or group who created the product or provided the service. It is this inherent element of authenticity that stirs our recognition that something wonderful has emerged to make the world a better place.

Great Work Is Everywhere

Some time ago, a few friends and I were eating at our favorite local restaurant where you order at the counter and the food is delivered to your table. As we waited for our meals, a member of our group lingered by the dessert counter, eyeing the luscious pastries.

One of the cooks who wasn't busy at the time came out from the line to give my friend a full explanation of each item. And then he said, "If you ever want anything special made, just let us know. We'll be happy to accommodate you."

My friend returned to our table, beaming over the interaction. For the remainder of our meal we watched this young cook. Even as the restaurant got very busy, he maintained his cheerful demeanor. Several times we noticed him extending himself to customers or co-workers—always with a big smile on his face.

Great Work Is Universal

As a course instructor, I also witnessed these attributes in many students who came from all over the world. Whether they hailed from India, Asia, Latin America, Europe, Canada, the United States or the Middle East, the outstanding ones were more alike than different—regardless of their backgrounds in fields as diverse as education, finance, sales or the military.

I particularly noticed that they put more effort into the classroom exercises and appeared to experience an unusual amount of satisfaction in the process. Their final evaluations indicated that they also received greater value from attending the course than their less-engaged fellow students.

Inner Wisdom Thrives in Connection

Observing these folks in action was probably when I first began to understand that the True Self thrives in connection.

Tapping into the "ineffable something" of intuition requires more than merely paying attention. We must engage. Take action. Be willing to change direction. Step off into the Unknown.

In order for inner wisdom to really make a difference in what

I do and how I "be" in that doing, I have found that I must treat
my Wise Inner Counselor as a trusted partner who desires only my
continued progress. For me, connecting with my inner wisdom is
like having a friend in high places. Work and life run a lot smoother
when I plug into that resource many times a day.

BRINGING SOUL TO YOUR WORK

The Wise Inner Counselor speaks directly to your soul.
If you want to do the great work that inner guidance
intends, your Soul Poetics™ is essential to the process.

The Ideal Partnership

Imagine your True Self as a most astute business partner who has invested heavily in your soul's future. This partner believes in you and your ability to fulfill your reason for being—which I have called your Soul Poetics. [3]

The term "poetics" comes from the root word that means to create. So the poetics of your soul is what you were born to bring into manifestation in this life. This process is also defined as "self-actualization" because you are making actual the abilities that reside in your soul as potential.

Work Is the Engine of Soul Poetics

Our particular creation need not be poetry, although I am convinced that each soul is poetical in its inner desire to contact more refined realms of being that are also very creative. Whatever our talents or preferences, we must put our soul gifts into action.

We accomplish nothing of lasting value in the world of form

unless our soul goes to work and completes the tasks that only we can do because of the specialized abilities we bring to the situation. Unless our souls are given challenges, problems to solve, people to help, our innate talents and attributes remain unrealized.

How Does the Partnership Work?

The soul of both men and women is by nature the receptive half of the partnership which receives the direction of the Wise Inner Counselor. Then the soul goes into action by contributing to the material world whatever it has been inspired to create.

In this interchange, greatness approaches perfection and may even achieve it. The deciding factor is the level of engagement of heart, mind, body and soul which the individual brings to bear in the doing.

From the perspective of the Wise Inner Counselor, the soul's most profound engagement is an activity of the greater Love for which it speaks.

Soul Makes All the Difference

Soul is the spark, the fire of the heart, that emanates from our best efforts. It is the ineffable quality we notice in the work of others.

Without soul, we are merely robots, programmed to achieve a sort of mechanical perfection through slavish obedience to rules that may or may not have been wisely inspired. The point is not so much the inception of the rules we obey. What matters is if we are aware of what we are doing and why we are doing it.

Soul work is infused with individual free will. People who choose to be exceptional in their endeavors are the ones who soar. They aim for new heights and achieve great results because they are free to do so.

Being Love in the Action of Doing

The Wise Inner Counselor and the soul work together creatively.

That is why I call the process of actualizing our inner gifts "Soul Poetics." To become who we are meant to be, we are inspired to engage in dynamic co-creation with our wise inner partner to solve the problems of being as well as the doing of our work.

This is the goal—no separation between our True Self, our outer awareness and our soul.

When this happens, when we are fully engaged in the work for which were born, the hours fly by. These are the times when we can say with my late father-in-law, a man who loved his work as a senior manager for Kodak, "I can't believe they pay me to do this."

These are also times when we and what we do are completely united in being our truest Self. We may even have what are called peak or mystical experiences in the midst of this work because we are so relaxed, so free from a sense of resistance or struggle that profound communion with more refined states of being naturally slip into our awareness.

These are moments when we become an example of Love in action, and our efforts unfold as if we were resting in the eye of a storm where all is sublimely peaceful.

PART TWO

Getting to the Heart of Great Work

Reflection 7

ENGAGING A NEW NORM

Those who would catch the wave of the future are challenged to incorporate a more profound presence of being into their doing.

Work as an Indicator of Life

The quality of our on-the-job experience will have immediate and far-reaching implications for our quality of life.

Many of us spend nearly seventy-five percent of our waking hours in work and work-related activities. In choosing our occupations, then, we do well to ensure that the hours we spend on the job serve to stimulate our minds, nurture our souls, open our hearts and elevate our spirits—in addition to paying to feed, clothe, house, transport and entertain us. Sometimes that can be a lot of work.

Many years ago I learned that the only way to move into a more desirable position was to love my way deeper into the one I had. Once I summoned renewed enthusiasm for my job, I frequently discovered fresh perspectives on the tasks involved, improved relationships with co-workers and creative solutions that I had not thought of before.

When my heart opened to new possibilities, I found myself once more engaged in the work at hand—and often in a new job.

Obstacles to Great Work

Have you ever felt bogged down at work by forces beyond your control? For many people, their jobs can be a struggle that wrings the energy and the joy right out of their lives. Sometimes even good jobs are too stressful.

I believe that most people want to bring their best efforts to work and life. Unfortunately, even the most dedicated employees are often stymied by cumbersome processes, antiquated bureaucracies, stressed-out managers or an alarming preponderance of a "just get it done" mentality that starts at the top of many organizations, perpetuating a culture of crisis, disrespect and hopelessness.

Experienced mentors seem pitifully scarce in these companies. Employers expect high performance, but many are unable or unwilling to explain it or train it. Instead, employees are thrown into challenging positions with minimal direction.

This is especially true for those new to management. Training may actually be blocked by those who are threatened by challenges to the status quo.

No Time to Improve?

While teaching a course on time management at the headquarters of a major insurance company, I was astonished that many of the attendees were repeatedly called out of class by their managers.

The general feedback at the end of the course was that the training was pointless because the managers "didn't have time" to learn new skills. And they either consciously or unconsciously sabotaged their employees' opportunity to improve how work was accomplished in their departments.

Transformational as the New Norm

Thankfully, things are changing. Despite challenges that have erupted internationally in recent times, we are seeing the emergence of new attitudes which have the capacity to shake up the old, outmoded ways of business as usual.

The importance of creating careers that are not separate from quality of life has never been greater. Effecting this change requires engagement by those who consider transformational outcomes the norm, not the exception.

Like the Total Professionals I met in my travels, these individuals place too high a value on their own time and potential to accept mediocrity in themselves or in their companies. They demand of their workplace the opportunity to do their best on a daily basis.

Of course, people with this perspective have always existed in every industry. The need for them has never been more acute, and I have a sense that they know it.

Technology Is Tangible

As a modern society, we like our technology. It is something we can put a finger on. When software creates errors, we reprogram or upgrade it. When hardware becomes outdated, we replace it. When a machine breaks, we install a new part. When a system is inefficient, we streamline it.

These are objects we can touch and control. They are things, and we are very accomplished at dealing with "thing" processes and structures. We can measure, calibrate and quantify them and their performance. Mechanical remedies for mechanical problems.

Still, a challenge for both employers and employees is that people are not things. They are massively complex human beings. Until we accept ourselves and others as the wonderfully creative, sometimes messy creatures we truly are, our workplaces and homes will continue to suffer a desperate incompleteness that ultimately affects entire communities and nations.

People Are Complicated

Employees are not mindless robots. The entire industrial/technological complex gets weak in the knees when people act out their inevitable emotions, wants, needs, values, beliefs, fears, illnesses and a thousand daily variables that threaten the stability of supply chains and production lines everywhere.

Even Henry Ford, who paid his workers the unheard-of salary of five dollars a day, is said to have complained, "Why is it when I hire a pair of hands, I also get a person?"

People are complicated. They are highly creative in their unpredictability. The good news is that increasing numbers of employers are paying attention because employee demands for personal consideration at work are likely only to multiply.

Offering Opportunities That Fit
Part of that consideration involves placing employees in positions where they can achieve their best results. While it is desirable to offer opportunities for advancement, they do need to be tailored to a person's top talents.

I once witnessed the unfortunate situation of a very talented computer programmer who was promoted to manage other pro-grammers. The poor man was so overwhelmed by "people issues" that he stayed in his office with the door closed for hours at a time.

Mercifully, he was relieved of that position, though not before chaos erupted in his department. If the man's supervisors had paid more attention to his actual talents and attributes as a human being, they would never have subjected him or his co-workers to such an experience.

What Are Companies Looking For?
Managers in my classes frequently reported that they were look-ing for mature, responsible, entrepreneurial attitudes in all of their candidates. Later they would train for the specific skills required in a particular job. But where do those attitudes come from?

It is difficult to train attitudes because they are the "inside" features—those unspoken, often unconscious attributes a person brings to the workplace. For individuals who value bringing soul to their work, these attributes are informed by a desire for work/life balance, personalized career tracks, flexible schedules, daily feedback and the opportunity to contribute their ideas immediately, not five or ten years from now.

I have come to see clearly that in order for work to be great, behaviors, skills and attitudes on the part of employees and employers must come together. When that happens, everybody wins.

Great Work Depends on Everybody

Time and again, my business class students bemoaned the dearth of effective leadership in their companies. However, after some spirited discussion, many admitted that they also could do better.

What I saw was the necessity for people at all levels of an organization to make balanced decisions, take appropriate action and create positive results within an atmosphere that meets today's changing expectations of what a meaningful life might be.

In our companies well-honed skills and effective attitudes that allow individuals to work productively alone as well as with other people are essential. An awareness that adheres to our core values, supports positive behaviors and travels with us wherever life and career may take us is irreplaceable.

Inner Wisdom Applies in Any Setting

While our Wise Inner Counselor may communicate with us in the language and symbolism of our culture and generation, the fact that we are capable of engaging inner wisdom applies to each of us, no matter who we are or where we come from.

My experience is that individuals who consistently access their inner wisdom as an adjunct to outer skills, knowledge and competencies are more alike than different, regardless of their training, culture or age.

Inner wisdom may be enhanced by formal education or apprenticeship. However, persistent curiosity about the world and the work we do in it, coupled with a willingness to learn from others, is far more likely to encourage the development of well-informed intuition in any setting.

The point is for employers and employees to acknowledge inner knowing as a viable competency and then to do the personal work necessary to improve the quality of that intuition.

Norms are changing. Attunement with our Wise Inner Counselor is one very effective way to be prepared for the transformation.

Reflection 8

EDUCATING FOR GREATNESS

*Trade schools, apprenticeships and certification
programs may be an answer for today's
students and for society as a whole.*

The Trades Are Still Necessary

One of the tragedies of today's world is that young people find themselves saddled with enormous debts for degrees that often do not prepare them for gainful employment.

While many companies still prefer a four-year degree, the value of those degrees is often questionable. I recently watched an interview with money manager Oliver Libby [4] who suggested that we must seriously reconsider what our traditional universities are teaching—or not teaching.

Libby points out that the United States is already suffering from a shortage of trained carpenters, plumbers, electricians and cybersecurity technicians. Many of these occupations do not require four-year degrees and pay very well.

As early as the late 1960's, the assistant superintendent of schools in Littleton, Colorado, was strongly advocating the benefits of a junior college education. At the same time our community was pushing a four-year college degree as the only reasonable path to advanced learning for its high school graduates.

The community's attitude was understandable. The Martin-Marietta company (later Lockheed-Martin) had recently located a new rocket and space shuttle development facility in the area. Many families moving to Littleton from the East Coast were scientists and technicians for whom traditional higher education was the norm.

Yet our local educator was adamant that society has as much need for skilled trades as for the sciences. At least in the near future, no matter how technologically advanced we become, we will still require the services of plumbers, carpenters and auto mechanics.

Benefits of a Two-Year Degree Program

When I worked for the Colorado Community College System, I saw first-hand the value and positive results achieved by this approach to education.

For one thing, introductory courses were taught by full professors, not graduate students. Class sizes were much smaller than at a large university, especially for first-year basic requirements.

Tuition was significantly lower than at a four-year college. Students could save money by living at home and commuting to class. The extra support of a smaller, community-college setting gave younger students more time to mature and explore their interests before facing the complexity of a large university or employment.

Faculty and administrators alike were very involved in the success of their diverse, often non-traditional student population.

A single class might include freshmen fulfilling their basic academic requirements, single parents who were pulling themselves out of poverty, ex-military personnel and those seeking retraining after losing their jobs. Bringing together a group with such varied backgrounds and perspectives enriched the learning experience for everyone.

The instructors I met were not burdened by a "publish or perish" mentality. They had more time and, frankly, more interest, in inspiring their students to graduate and find their place in a well-paying job.

At the time, I was especially gratified to discover that a number of the community college presidents and vice presidents taught at least one course per term so they could remain knowledgeable about student needs and preferences. I hope they still do.

Education's Missing Ingredient

Soon after I began teaching corporate management classes, I became aware that a welcoming heart was what many of the attendees seemed most to need—especially some of the younger students who arrived with a cynical attitude they had picked up from their peers, the media or at school.

The courses I taught had more to do with solving "people" issues, and those issues were often very burdensome to many of the attendees. I quickly discovered that the most important thing I could do at the outset was to create an environment that was conducive to exploring difficult topics.

During the first morning's introductory session, I focused on helping the attendees feel trusted and encouraged to take a chance on experimenting with approaches to work and life that I knew were going to stretch them during the course activities.

Hearts and Minds Opened

Without fail, as we moved into the first afternoon session, a positive atmosphere began percolating throughout the classroom. People relaxed and opened up. Class discussions became more courageous. Insights were more profound.

Sharing grew richer and more practical as learning activities encouraged partners and small groups to be genuinely helpful to one another. Even the cynics (and there were always a few) started to have more fun.

Giving Inner Guidance a Chance

I remember one young National Guard lieutenant who sat with his arms folded in the back of class during the entire first morning. I was conducting a special on-site course in creative problem solving, and he was required to attend with his unit for an entire weekend.

My intuition told me very clearly to let him find his way. I was confident that the course material (which was excellent) and my openness would produce more positive results than pushing him to participate. I simply told him I understood that he was essentially a prisoner in my classroom and that he was free to participate or not, as he chose.

By the end of the first day, his arms unfolded. By early afternoon of the second day he began to ask questions and join in some of the learning activities.

By the third and final day of instruction he had become the most enthusiastic participant. When he shook my hand after class, he thanked me for trusting him and told me he was glad he had attended. He also gave me the best evaluation of anyone in his unit.

We Thrive When People Are Passionate About Work

My experience with individuals like this young lieutenant confirmed my belief that people will be naturally effective, creative and passionate about their professions when we support their inner guidance and fully engage our own.

When we encourage our young people to partner with their inner wisdom, which operates through the heart as well as the head, I am convinced they will find their way to the type of education they require for the occupations that suit the natural gifts of their souls.

Won't that be great!

Reflection 9

BUILDING TRUST

Building trust requires effort and it takes time,
although perhaps not as long as you might think.

Testing Our Ability to Trust

Ideally, as young children, we may frolic in an unselfconscious cocoon of spontaneous inspiration, completely at home in a secure environment that points us as far as our imaginations can carry us.

Yet as we begin to grow up, the development of our own critical mind (plus the opinions and demands of authority figures) sows seeds of doubt to cloud that clarity. So we begin to question our ability to trust circumstances involving our teachers, families, friends, co-workers, employers or employees—all those individuals who make up our personal and professional communities.

Learning Trust in Common Causes

For many of us, the organizations in which we work frame a primary experience of trusting relationships.

Our associations with those companies (or with groups we join for common cause) are often defined by formal, written agreements such as employment contracts.

Even more pervasive and powerful are the implied agreements—the assumptions we make about the rights we claim for ourselves and those we extend to others.

These mostly unwritten rules weave the fabric of family, community and organizational character, and create the flavor of their cultures. The sweetness or bitterness of those cultures flows from the presence or absence of their essential ingredient: Trust.

Trust Is Vital

Trust is one of the most fragile elements in human relationships and potentially one of the strongest. It is the currency with which we create our relationships, credibility, reputation, effectiveness and, ultimately, our legacy.

The rewards of trust are manifold and the penalties for its betrayal may last a lifetime or longer.

Trust is as durable as its next ten expressions and as frail as a single lapse. Once broken, it is difficult to repair. Yet trust has the power to hold millions together—so entrancing is its effect on the human psyche.

We accomplish nothing without trust. With it, we can save the world. Without it, even the best ideas go begging for a hearing.

Trust is the ultimate reciprocal quality an individual may possess. I have observed that the extent to which we are trusted is in direct proportion to the amount of trust we extend to others.

Or, we could say that the extent to which we trust others is in direct proportion to how trustworthy we, ourselves, are.

The Power of Trustworthy Leadership

In his essay, "Prudence," Ralph Waldo Emerson said, "Trust men and they will be true to you; treat them greatly, and they will show themselves great."[5]

In my experience, leaders and managers who naturally trust others also see themselves as consistent, dependable and honorable—undergirded by principles and core values that inform their behavior. They convey trustworthiness, and that is what they receive from others. Likewise, those who proclaim that people must earn their trust also tend to get what they expect.

Cultures of fear and distrust eventually paralyze institutions. Top performers leave and others merely survive—in both cases withholding their talents, expertise and insights that otherwise could have created a robust organization.

Conversely, dynamic departments that really hum (even within a dysfunctional company) are run by managers who foster trust in their employees and encourage them to do their best.

The resulting high energy, enthusiasm and productivity spring from a supportive environment that promotes self-expression, collaboration and creativity, which are the hallmarks of great work and deep connection with the Wise Inner Counselor.

I know this to be true because I have worked in both kinds of environments.

A Willingness to Be Vulnerable

My husband and I once attended a weekend seminar that included a community-building exercise. This activity revealed a vital factor in creating trust between individuals and within a larger group—the willingness to be vulnerable.

The facilitator asked us to divide into small groups. Then she presented a series of phrases that each individual was to speak aloud, taking turns around the group several times before the next phrase was introduced.

The first phrase got things going as we stated: "What I want you to know about me is...."

We smilingly revealed ourselves as football fans or lovers of chocolate or dogs. Our answers became more serious as we went on to identify severe illnesses, difficult behavioral challenges, fears, losses, hopes and dreams.

Strengthening the Bonds of Trust

Each round went still deeper into personal experiences and ranged wider in variety. As increasingly tender information or funny insights were appreciatively received, we eagerly continued the exercise.

In the space of ten minutes, a little community began to form—based on the experience that embarrassing or heartbreaking facts about ourselves would be met with respect and openness.

Commonalities emerged to strengthen the bonds that were developing. Each of us identified several personal strengths and weaknesses, and we offered areas of expertise and special talents that could be useful to the group.

At that point, had we been charged with completing an actual project, we could have immediately brought those resources to bear with potentially very positive results.

This exercise was an invigorating experience and demonstrated how easy it is to build trust within a group if all members are willing and able to risk self-revelation while meeting the vulnerabilities of others with good will.

Most people have the ability and the desire to create this type of deep, personal trust—which is why it can form so quickly in a supportive environment. The difficulty lies in maintaining that trust when political, economic or social forces alter the environment and challenge the principles and core values upon which it was built.

Acquiring a Taste for Trust

Have you ever had the feeling that something was going on behind your back, but you did not know what it could be?

Sometimes we "get a feeling" about a person or situation, which may be our Wise Inner Counselor warning us. We should certainly heed those warnings.

We humans do tend to a natural uneasiness with unfamiliar circumstances. If we hold a strong intention of creating trust in ourselves and others, we do well to manage those suspicions.

For example, when I conduct workshops in person or online, the first group activity sets ground rules for confidentiality. We also establish norms designed to prevent participants from intruding upon others, no matter how well-meaning their suggestions may be.

In this way, attendees collaborate on creating an environment of trust, which allows them to feel more comfortable discussing the difficult issues they hope to resolve in class.

Sharing a Meal Can Build Trust

While conducting a nine-month leadership academy for the Colorado Community College System, the participants and I learned the value of sharing at least one meal together during the weekend—usually on a Friday night preceding Saturday's full day of training.

The opportunity those dinners provided invariably led to open sharing of personal information as the educators put aside job titles, degrees and expectations. The result was a remarkable amount of trust building between different factions, some of whom had been at odds with one another for years.

By the end of a single meal, creative ideas were flowing, problems were being solved and best practices were emerging that would have required hours to uncover in a workshop.

When the participants arrived on Saturday morning, they were eager to learn together. They even created more challenging exercises than I had designed. Friendships were forged and bonds cemented that endured long after the academy concluded at the end of the school year.

There were more than a few tears shed in the closing ceremony. Such was the effect of well-earned trust.

Lessons in Trust from the Leadership Academy

Here are some of the most important lessons the participants and I learned about creating and maintaining trust:

- If you want to establish trusting relationships with others, pay attention to them.

- Spend time with them and actively listen to what they say. Look them in the eye and tell them the truth.

- Follow up with actions that are consistent with fairness and good will. Let them know you understand their concerns and proactively support their best efforts.

The little things are what build up trust. An occasional grand gesture is not the same as frequent, small interactions that convey the message, "I care what happens to you. I am aware of what you are doing. I appreciate your point of view. I value our relationship."

Trust that is built upon this foundation of honesty and genuine care is resilient and flexible, able to weather occasional storms of adversity.

Well-established trust is also more likely to heal misunderstandings than is a leader's mere appearance of interest that is based on motivational slogans or once-a-year performance evaluations.

Nurturing Trust

Generating trust requires effort and it takes time. For some it is an acquired taste. Ten years of working with the same people may be needed to establish trust, or it can emerge in a ten-minute exercise.

Building trust also depends on the integrity, intensity and intimacy of the conversation, and on how we nurture our relationships over time—including the vital relationship with our own Wise Inner Counselor.

Reflection 10

AMPLIFYING TRUST IN TIME

Honoring each other's time is the foundation of every
positive relationship—business or personal.

Life Is All About Time

If you have ever lost a loved one or a beloved pet, you know that time is really all we have in this life. And look at what we do with this precious resource: We spend time, kill time, lose time, waste time. We try to keep time, save time or make time.

If we are bored, time may drag on. If we are engaged in what we are doing, time flies by. Minutes, hours, days, weeks, months or years may be a burden. But when our time is up, nothing else matters except how meaningfully we have used our time.

At its most fundamental, life on earth is all about time, which is why people take such exception to theirs being wasted.

When we are late, we are putting our own preferences above those who rely on us.

When we show up on time we are saying, "I value you and I honor our time together. I want to help us make the most of it so we can accomplish something truly fine."

My associates in the staffing industry know this lesson all too well. They would have far fewer gray hairs if their applicants for temporary employment understood the importance of showing up on time.

Different Perceptions of Time

When I was doing business training, I gained a vivid appreciation for the fact that not everyone approaches time in the same way. One way in which we build trust is by respecting those differences.

Time is money to some. Others emphasize being on time as well as on budget. People time is highly valued by many. Those who are occupied with ideas and innovations may have a somewhat loose concept of time.

We lose people's respect when our problems with time management negatively affect how and when they do their own work. Mind-numbing meetings, disregard for colleagues' schedules and chronic lateness all send a message that we do not value them or their contribution.

People understand that time is opportunity and they begin to distrust those who waste it. I have seen an entire reorganization project fail—due, at least in part, to one key person's problem with managing his own time and, hence, that of others.

A Cautionary Tale of Time

One of the most interesting and challenging positions I ever held was that of assistant to Sam, a people-oriented management consultant who was hired to re-engineer the company where I worked.

The organization was mired in a cumbersome hierarchical structure that had resulted in an entrenched silo mentality. Many processes were beset with convoluted feedback loops so that few projects were completed.

At first it seemed that Sam was the perfect person for the job. He loved people and was dedicated to finding ways to unleash their creativity and productivity. Expectations were high that his innate belief in employees' talents would turn things around.

The biggest expectation was that he would change a company culture that had a rather fluid relationship with meeting or event starting times due to factors for which no one was really to blame.

Unfortunately, Sam proved to be equally loose with time. He frequently chose to extend a one-on-one personnel interview when a dozen executive team members were waiting to begin an all-day meeting on the future of the entire organization.

His decision was a tough call because individual employees were eager for a hearing, and Sam firmly believed in leaving the "ninety-and-nine" to seek out the one lost in the thicket. Predictably, however, the "ninety-and nine" grew testy and returned to their old ways of compensating for one another's tardiness.

Meetings began later and later. Team unity was undermined. Sam lost the buy-in and valuable input of some of his primary stakeholders who concluded that things really were not going to change after all.

Sam had many great ideas, but most came to naught because he did not build trust in the most foundational element of organizational behavior—respect for other people's time.

Freedom from Crisis

My concept of time management changed from crisis to flow many years ago when my department head discovered Stephen Covey's book *The 7 Habits of Highly Effective People*. [6]

Covey's idea of allotting time to do what is important, not only urgent, precipitated my boss's epiphany. He bought copies of the book for everybody in the office and declared that we were no longer going to operate in crisis mode.

Several weeks were required for us to train ourselves and our clients to plan ahead. But once we started setting aside time to focus on new ideas or projects that had never come to the top of our in-boxes, the number and frequency of emergency calls decreased.

In fact, a wave of innovation broke out. Within this freshly proactive environment editors, technicians, support personnel and managers took time to rethink their jobs.

Informal discussions led to formal problem-solving sessions. Individuals developed innovations that saved the company scores of man-hours and thousands of dollars. Everybody had more fun at work and the level of mutual trust soared.

Correcting Chronic Lateness

A wise friend kindly taught me a quick remedy for chronic lateness: Identify what particular events you are late for and what causes you to be delayed. For example, pointing out my theater background, he suggested that perhaps I enjoyed the drama of making an entrance with everyone watching.

I am happy to say that I have since broken the habit of being late. In fact, I have an associate who says he can set his watch by me because I always show up on time.

Consider your own habits. Do you enjoy the adrenalin rush of driving too fast or running to catch your train at the last minute? Or are you afraid of what may happen when you arrive?

The First Requirement

I once was part of a selection committee for a high-level administrative assistant position. One candidate demanded to be seen, despite the fact that she was fifteen minutes late for the mandatory exam which preceded the formal interview.

She did not realize that punctuality was the first and most essential requirement of her being considered for the position. Her other qualifications were irrelevant in the light of her tardiness.

We learned later that she was afraid of taking the exam and, instead, hoped to talk her way into the job. Her ruse did not work, which was unfortunate, because she was otherwise very qualified for the position.

Inner Wisdom Is Always on Time

Timing is everything for the Wise Inner Counselor. The consequences of not immediately following its guidance can be costly. As I happened to be working on this reflection, a friend told me the following story:

> Yesterday I had several errands to accomplish. My inner wisdom made it very clear that I needed to get out and back early in the day.
>
> Unfortunately, I ended up waiting for delivery of a package that was late. Instead of leaving the house when I knew I was supposed to, I allowed myself to be delayed until mid-afternoon.
>
> Everything went smoothly until I was waiting to turn right out of the grocery store parking lot. I was second in line with no way to avoid the car that suddenly rolled right into my bumper.
>
> Fortunately, the damage was minimal. The woman driver was very apologetic and embarrassed at her laxity. She had been distracted while looking for something in her passenger seat and had taken her foot off the brake.
>
> I knew I was not supposed to be where I was at that point in time. My failure to trust my inner wisdom resulted in time and money wasted.
>
> As it turned out, I could have run my errands as directed and been safely back home before the package I was waiting for actually arrived. My intuition is always on time.

Operating in the Present

In the adventure that is life, the time that matters is now. We can waste time by living in the past or the future, but neither really exists. The past is gone and the future is yet to be determined.

What matters is how we fill our time in this moment. Now is when we start and now is when we finish. Now is when we make decisions. Now is when we succeed or fail.

Now is like money in the bank. As long as today exists, we have opportunity to invest some of today's now to fund tomorrow's activities—to multiply our talents, to share our gifts and to enjoy the return on our investment of all the nows that have gone before.

Every day offers a new opportunity to relax into the joyful present. In this now, fewer crises arise and more events can unfold naturally in work and life—almost as if today does contain enough hours and minutes for us to work in sync with inner guidance and accomplish the desired results on time.

Reflection 11

WILLING AND ABLE TO RESPOND

To respond is to give answer, to reply.
One original meaning is to promise.

We Will Be There

At home and at work we give answer to both spoken and unspoken requests for us to honor our community, protect its integrity, see to its safety and prosperity, watch over its areas of vulnerability and elevate our collective humanity to its noblest expression.

We are willing to put "our lives, our fortunes and our" [7] on the line for the sake of those in our care. In the case of first responders, their promise is: "We will be there when you need us."

Reflecting on Accountability

If I am accountable, I own my thoughts, words and deeds. I am not a victim and I believe that much of what happens to me is a result of forces I have set in motion. Circumstances I do not particularly like probably still have more to do with my attitudes and perceptions than with the actions of others.

When I see my reflection in the mirror, do I ask: "What have I thought, said or done to create my current circumstance? Am I not where I am today as a result of decisions and choices I have made?"

Observing myself and others convinces me that we actually do what we want, even if we do not like what we are doing. For example, going to a job we dislike is still preferable to not being employed. We may complain about the work, the boss or our co-workers, but ultimately we are accountable for the quality of our experience by how we choose to respond.

Accountability Works Both Ways

Accountability requires empowerment. I cannot be accountable for my actions if I do not have the authority to take actions that I deem appropriate. If I view challenges as opportunities to do my best, I must have the autonomy to act accordingly.

Authority figures who erect road blocks that prevent their employees from taking responsible action are not allowing them to be accountable. The employees may find themselves assuming the blame, but they are not at fault. That responsibility lies with those who stifled their ability to respond.

Of course, one remedy is for the employees to propose to their supervisors ways in which they can be more effective by allowing them to provide their customers with timely solutions.

This is the kind of common-sense response that creates great work—when we resist the temptation to blame others and, instead, listen for the unique answer that is just waiting for us to turn within.

Accountability in Action

Recently a close friend was in the process of selling her home. To schedule showings her real estate agent engaged the services of a company that coordinates showings for multiple Realtors.

When a request for a showing came in, the company would immediately contact my friend. She would then confirm or deny the appointment or request an alternate time.

If a problem or question arose, she would call the scheduler who was empowered to solve the problem—on the spot.

The result was a happy seller, satisfied potential buyers and many relieved Realtors because the schedulers were accountable for excellent results and had the authority to achieve them.

Changing Attitudes About Accountability

Here is a not-so-positive story from a frustrated computer teacher whose students believed that their life circumstances exempted them from normal academic accountabilities such as turning in assignments or even attending class:

> When I was growing up, there was a junkyard close to my home. My father barred me and my brothers from playing there for fear we would hurt ourselves on sharp metal objects that could cause tetanus.
>
> Of course, we sneaked into the junkyard anyway and cut ourselves, our wounds requiring stitches and tetanus shots. Our dad was furious and we were grounded for weeks following.
>
> These days, I would expect the parents of some of my students to sue the junkyard for not putting up a sign warning kids that it might be dangerous.

Accounting for Our Edge

We tend to think of people who do great work as hard-driving workaholics who thrive on 18-hour days. But for most of us, extreme schedules eventually take a toll on our judgment and performance.

The ability to respond appropriately, then, has much to do with caring for our physical and mental health so our faculties are sharp and responsive.

Professional athletes or dancers will tell you that success is all in the preparation and the practice. You do not sink a fifty-foot putt by accident or execute a flawless pirouette by chance.

The apparent ease with which these professionals perform

belies the years of hard work they put into honing their skills, disciplining their minds and caring for their bodies so they can respond with effortless grace. They are accountable for achieving superior results, and they work hard at it every day.

Responding Greatly in the Hour of Need

Learning to answer the inner and outer call to appropriate action is no less rigorous a discipline.

The extent to which we function in that flow at home and at work is the extent to which we can be relied upon to respond appropriately, here and now. We practice listening for the present moment's inspiration to offer our best efforts in any situation.

Exactly as US Airways pilot Chesley ("Sully") Sullenberger did on January 15, 2009 when he landed an Airbus A320 on New York's Hudson River after hitting a flock of geese and losing power in both engines.

Incredibly, all 155 passengers and crew survived, due to Captain Sullenberger's response that combined extraordinary technical savvy, emotional poise and well-honed human intuition.

Preparation Matters

Sully had been flying since he was a boy. He knew airplanes inside and out, including the big jet he was flying out of LaGuardia Airport in New York City on a crisp, cold January afternoon.

"I knew what the A320 could do," he later explained to the National Transportation Safety Board (NTSB) investigators—a fact substantiated by his almost immediate decision to turn off the autopilot and fly the plane himself.

Nobody had ever trained for the scenario in which Sully and his co-pilot, Jeff Skiles, found themselves—which could have meant panic in the cockpit. Instead, they pulled out an emergency checklist and began the systematic process of readying the plane for impact.

Throughout his career as a pilot, Sully had encountered many dangerous situations—in both real and simulated scenarios. As an airline safety expert, he knew that he and his crew could rely on standard procedures to keep their naturally reactive survival responses under control.

But he did not rely on a checklist sequence to determine how to execute the actual water landing—and that is the reason all 155 passengers and crew survived.

Captain Chesley "Sully" Sullenberger III visiting the Virtual Motion Simulator at NASA Ames Research Center, Moffett Field Calif.
Photo Credit: NASA Ames Research Center / Eric James

Trusting Intuition

The movie about the event dubbed by the media as "The Miracle on the Hudson" reveals the captain's focused demeanor and confidence in his years of experience and training when he matter-of-factly states to the NTSB investigating panel, "I was sure I could do it."

Then he shocks them by admitting that there was no time for complex analysis or trajectory computations. Once he decided to land on the Hudson, "I eye-balled it," he says.

In other words, Sully ignored all distractions—and there were plenty, as the cockpit recording replay makes clear later in the movie. In that seminal moment, he focused his total attention on guiding the huge airliner into a perfect water landing on the Hudson River. In a televised interview the real Sully summed up the event:

> One way of looking at this might be that for 42 years I've been making small, regular deposits in this bank of experience, education and training. And on January 15, the balance was sufficient so that I could make a very large withdrawal. [8]

The X factor was Sully's quietly confident ability to summon all of his faculties in combination with the intuitive force of his Wise Inner Counselor to compute the perfect coordinates for an unprecedented outcome.

If you have not seen the film, I recommend that you do. Sully's statement, "My aircraft" and his copilot's answer, "Your aircraft" is one of the most powerful scenes in the movie that contains many compelling moments.

Others Also Responded

Another highlight of the movie is its depiction of the flotilla of New York Waterways ferries and boats from the US Coast Guard, New York Fire Department and others who immediately came on scene.

They arrived within minutes to rescue the passengers and crew who had evacuated the plane as it took on water and now were stranded on its wings and in life rafts.

The captain of the first ferry boat to arrive, who actually

played himself in the film, saved over fifty people in less than ten minutes, whisking them back to shore where ambulances and land-based first responders saw to their safety and medical needs.

Other maritime crews likewise took action as their years of water rescue training had prepared them. Because of their clear thinking, knowledge and discipline, the entire operation took place in less than thirty minutes.

In the days and weeks that followed, the rescuers were duly honored for their selflessness in coming to the aid of their fellow men, women and children.

Many surely would have perished if "We will be there when you need us" had not been a core value and fundamental principle of those who responded greatly in the time of need.

Rescue efforts that saved all 155 lives of
US Airways Flight 1549 passengers and crew.
Credit: REUTERS/Brendan McDermid, Adobe images.

PART THREE

Paying Attention to Great Work

Reflection 12

FOCUSING ON
WHAT'S HAPPENING

When I say that top performers are focused,
many people will ask, "Focused on what?"
To which I answer, "Exactly. Focus on 'what'."

A Fortunate Encounter

During my years as a corporate instructor, I taught a course on critical thinking and creative problem solving. It contained a module on troubleshooting that advocated asking the question "what?" to determine the cause of a problem.

As chance would have it, while on a flight from New York to Washington, D. C., I gained some valuable insight into just how essential focusing on "what?" can be.

Troubleshooting Asks "What?"

I happened to sit next to a clear-eyed gentleman who turned out to be one of four national troubleshooting experts who could be called in to handle serious problems at large utility installations anywhere in the United States. He agreed that asking "what?" was his primary investigative tool. Here is what he told me:

If I were to say things like "Why did this happen? Who is responsible? What were you thinking?" people would clam up. They would get defensive, especially if my tone were the least bit accusatory.

Instead, I ask them, "What was happening right before the problem occurred? What did you notice when the system went down? What was different about this day than any other?"

When I focus on fact-finding, even the culprits will usually come forward with the information we need to solve the problem and put systems in place to prevent its re-occurrence.

After this encounter, I began asking "what?" questions more frequently in my personal life as well as in the classroom. My ability to focus on priorities definitely improved, and my students benefited from the clarity they experienced in class.

Do You Know What Is Expected of You?

Have you ever been in a situation when you suddenly stopped and asked yourself, "What am I doing here?" Or "What do other people think I should be doing here?"

The author of the critical thinking course developed an effective process for teasing out some answers to those questions:

- Draw a circle on a large piece of paper.

- On the outside are things that you cannot control (weather).

- On the inside of the circle are people and other factors over which you have some influence.

- Interview those people to find out what they really think about your project, your role(s) and theirs.

- Adjust accordingly.

Identifying What Is Really Happening

Here is the story shared by a course attendee who used the process when adding a bathroom in his basement—a project he thought his family all agreed was a good idea:

> On the inside of my project circle were the names of my wife, Julia, our 14-year-old daughter, Cathy, and 10-year-old son, Aaron. I figured everybody was on board with the bathroom project, but decided to follow the process anyway.
>
> Honestly, I was shocked by the responses. My wife wasn't happy about having workmen in and out of the house over the course of several months and was beginning to regret her earlier enthusiasm for the bathroom.
>
> Our daughter, Cathy, was thrilled because it meant she could move downstairs into her own space. That change actually concerned me because I worried about her online activities being more difficult to supervise.
>
> It took some coaxing to discover why Aaron was upset about the project. He finally confided to his mother his resentment about Cathy now "owning" the basement, which he had previously considered his domain.
>
> I had thought that my role was merely to pay the bills and offer some occasional input on design or materials selection. Now I discovered that "peacemaker" was my primary function.
>
> Over the next few weeks, I negotiated comprises between Julia and the contractor for downstairs access through the back door. Cathy and I had a serious talk about Internet security and searching safety.
>
> I mediated a heated conversation between Cathy and Aaron about shared "ownership" of the basement. I had to reassure the neighbors that the demolition dumpster

was temporary and that construction workers weren't going to block their driveways.

The process required far more time and attention than I had anticipated. But it was certainly preferable to the emotional outbursts and arguments that might have erupted without each person feeling they had been heard and their concerns addressed up front.

The experience really changed how I perceive my roles at work and what I focus on, especially if significant changes are taking place in my company or department.

Nowadays I pay a lot more attention to what is happening around me in all aspects of my life—and to what those circumstances mean to others involved. It's great to have the family united again.

Reflection 13

WHAT IS YOUR OCCUPATION?

What occupies the majority of your time and attention?
You may be surprised when you observe yourself.

Where Is Your Focus?

We usually think of an occupation as what someone does for a living. But what if we allow the word to point us to the thoughts and feelings that occupy the majority of our attention?

The consequences for not being focused on the matter at hand can be serious, as I discovered while conducting a team-building workshop for a compliance department overseeing federal grants.

The Mismatched Team

This group was tasked with assuring that government funds were properly allocated to support community college tech-ed programs, and they were having problems meeting objectives.

Compliance work is extremely detailed, generates a lot of paperwork and requires constant vigilance and monitoring. These responsibilities demanded that the team members function together—in the office—to update reports on a regular basis.

Nobody on that team (not one person!) enjoyed the tasks that their positions required. They were more occupied with the social and innovative aspects of their jobs—although few of their innovations ever got past the idea stage. The most seriously preoccupied person in the group was the department head, who spent as much time as possible away from the office on field visits.

After this workshop, several team members made a conscious effort to focus on the requirements of their jobs. Others, including the department head, immediately requested transfers to positions more in alignment with their preferences.

Practicing Situational Awareness

In addition to concentrating on what we are doing, we are wise to be aware of the environment in which we act and the consequences of our actions.

Many human errors occur because people become desensitized to their environment. They may be so occupied with a single task that they fail to notice a change in the environment. Or their distraction may set up an accident for unsuspecting passers-by.

That is what nearly happened to my husband, who often rode his bicycle home from work when the weather was pleasant.

One afternoon Stephen came home visibly upset. A maintenance worker had pulled his truck across the bike path at an angle and not fully onto the shoulder. As my husband came zipping along, he suddenly realized that the truck tailgate was open and sticking out into the path.

Fortunately, there were no other cyclists close by, so he was able to swerve around the truck, safely stop his bike and close the tailgate for the worker who was nowhere in sight. Clearly, the man was unaware of the hazard he had created. At that moment, the total scope of his work was not his occupation.

Asking the True Self "What?"

I have learned that sometimes the most important question I can ask of my Wise Inner Counselor is: "What do I need to know right now?" Or "What am I not seeing that I should?"

For many years, I did not always remember to ask. But when I did, the response was often astonishing. Answers to specific questions I had not known to ask were immediately forthcoming.

Words of encouragement, insights into current projects, even predictions of future events spilled onto the pages of my journal or simply flowed into my awareness.

Nowadays, I strive to maintain what some might call a state of listening grace that is always open to hearing inner wisdom tell me, "This is what you need to know right now."

And I ask anyway. The Wise Inner Counselor nearly always has more to say. That additional "what?" becomes my very focused occupation.

Reflection 14

ENGAGING IN EXCELLENCE
IN ANY OCCUPATION

*Maria Montessori understood that when
children learn to love to do well, they do.*

The Inner Teacher

Maria Montessori was the ultimate champion of what she called a child's inner teacher. She understood that children who are allowed to engage in what interests them naturally pursue excellence as a way of life that is energetic, positive, inspired and confident.

She emphasized that the inner teacher is not a creature of mechanical perfection. This presence lives in the heart and acts from within, prompting each of us to give our best effort—from childhood through adulthood. When children are taught to engage inner guidance, their souls' innate desire for excellence emerges.

Giving a Perfect Effort

I recently watched the movie *When the Game Stands Tall* based on a true story of the football team that won 151 straight games between 1992 and 2003 for De La Salle High School in Concord, California. [9]

Head Coach Bob Ladouceur's secret was in not focusing on winning. Instead he asked his players to give a perfect effort on every play, "from snap to whistle." As long as they gave their best and supported each other in that pursuit of full engagement, the team went on winning.

Excellence was their passion. Perfection was in the effort—not in focusing on creating an impossibly perfect result. In fact, the idea of winning every game became a distraction, especially when fans and some players became obsessed with "The Streak."

When Work Is Play

We are naturally excellent and engaged when we love what we are doing. Those tasks become a deep expression of our True Self in an activity that we make uniquely our own. An accurate clue to that innate excellence is found in discovering the "work" that is really our "play."

I remember an engineer at a Texaco office where I was a receptionist. As he walked by my desk on his way to the kitchen to dump a cold cup of coffee, he ruefully remarked, "I don't know why I bother to carry a full cup of coffee back to my office in the morning. I take a couple of sips, start working at my drawing board—and before I know it, it's 10:00 a.m. and the coffee's cold."

Clearly, this was a man who loved his work, and his enthusiasm was inspiring. He wasn't boastful about how hard or well he worked—although he put in a lot of effort and was very talented in his field. He was just a guy who loved being an engineer and who did not waste time on distractions—even his morning cup of coffee.

Engaging in Excellence Is Risky

If you want to be excellent, you must risk being terrible. Practice may eventually make perfect, but it can take a really long time with a lot of errors along the way. (Edison reportedly discovered over one thousand ways *not* to make a light bulb.)

When I was in theater, I used to love rehearsals for a new play or musical when we experimented with line readings and staging to test what worked and what didn't. Some of our ideas were awkward. Others we kept and enhanced as the show's run progressed.

As a writer, I know I am going to be doing more editing and re-writing than initial composition. The important part of the process is to capture the initial ideas and then refine them—as many times as necessary to make clear what I am trying to say.

The true hallmark of excellence is not its perfection but its comfort with imperfection while seeking the desired outcome. Excellence is willing to make mistakes to discover what works best. It is organic, dynamic and often unpredictable in its ability to change direction when the present course is not achieving great results.

Daring to Improve

For years I worked with world-class performers and technicians in theater and audio/video production. We took risks by daring to improve. We pushed each other to top our previous achievements. In the process we created an environment in which everyone understood that true excellence takes relentless practice and focus.

Ours was a high-wire act where failure in the final production was not an option. The show, indeed, had to go on. I have performed with a raging fever, a cut foot and laryngitis. I have walked off the back of an elevated stage, cut my head open on a piece of scenery and still managed to sing, dance and deliver my lines on cue. (Thankfully, these were all separate incidents.)

I was not alone in those feats. My colleagues and I were not always perfect, but we were fully engaged in delivering a perfect effort. And the feeling was exhilarating. There were times that being on stage was for many of us a transcendent experience because of the synergistic connection we felt between our own inner reality, the other performers and the audience.

By focusing on being fully engaged in our work, we achieved vivid moments of excellence. The experience was perfect.

FINANCIALS MATTER

*There is nothing like running your own business
to help you pay attention to how you allocate all
of your resources—especially the monetary ones.*

"Every Decision Is a Financial Decision"

When the leader of the non-profit organization I worked for made that statement, I was skeptical. After all, we were working for high ideals that were supported by a generous international membership. So why was money an issue?

Now, as a business owner, I understand. My boss knew that we had to be frugal with our resources and mindful of wisely investing donations to further the cause for which they had been given.

Today I can see that everything I do has financial implications. And despite my personal tendency to consider the "money" issues last, the principle is clear. Those little decisions to save or spend add up.

Business Creates Wealth for People

When I worked as a video producer for a leadership program on PBS Business Channel, one of the most interesting thought leaders we met was former Schering-Plough CEO Robert W. Collins.

Collins defined creating wealth as the special function of businesses, both large and small. No other sector of society does so, and wealth is the engine that drives a culture's progress—releasing individuals from dawn-to-dusk toil for mere subsistence to pursuing a life of meaning and fulfillment.

For the People, By the People

Collins and others like him believe that the company is for people, not the reverse. They understand that poverty keeps people poor in spirit and in thought, not only in things.

The hungry do not easily invent. The downtrodden do not philosophize. And the jobless are hard-pressed to contribute to the betterment of society if they do not have employment in which to engage their souls in the work they were born for.

This is not to say that people in dire situations do not create innovative solutions to improve their circumstances. We know that necessity is indeed the mother of invention.

Yet it is also true that reducing people to subsistence conditions, especially by eliminating their opportunity to pursue meaningful work, seriously limits their ability to engage in the type of soul growth and advancement they innately desire.

Everybody Owns the Results

A dynamic communications director I worked with said of his former boss, "He was not an easy man to work for, but he took the time to give meaningful praise. And when he did that for me, I gave 180 percent. Everybody in the office felt the same."

That was a financial decision as well an example of wise leadership. Imagine the positive implications of motivating your employees (or colleagues) to give 180 percent. If you, as an employee, feel a sense of ownership and empowerment in your company, do you not automatically take better care of the company's resources, facilities and customers?

That has always been my experience, and my workshop attendees agreed that they are more financially responsible when they feel appreciated as valued members of the organization.

Generosity and a Sense of Abundance

I once had the good fortune to attend a weekend seminar by Thomas Leonard—a prolific author and the person who, until his untimely death in 2003, almost single-handedly created and then popularized the life-coaching industry.

One of the most successful individuals in the early twenty-first century, Leonard trained thousands of coaches based on a model of personal and financial generosity. He practically gave away his expertise and still became a millionaire while demonstrating how creating "a life, not a lifestyle" could lead to dramatic financial stability, professional success and personal well-being.

He was generous with his time and knowledge as he gathered like-minded colleagues around him to build a vast network in an unbelievably short period of time. The legacy he left continues to provide inspiration and practical resources through a financial engine that generates wealth for thousands of individuals and their businesses.

Jack Canfield proved the same benefits of being generous. When he first published *Chicken Soup for the Soul,* he gave away countless copies, spoke for free and made himself available to help others. Now he is the preeminent success principles coach who continues to be a very generous person. [10]

Believing in Enough

Thomas Leonard inspired me to believe that when we are in the flow of our own energy economy, there is enough time, enough money, enough clients, enough opportunity.

Each one of us has an allotment of time, talent and other inner and outer resources that we are free to use in any occupation. The key to creating a life of meaning and fulfillment is to realize that none of these is infinite. We must spend them wisely.

What is infinite, however, is the universe we inhabit. We in the industrialized world exist in the midst of astonishing abundance. As long as we adhere to core values, principles of ethics and just stewardship of what we have been given, that abundance may continue to be available to us.

We may not have as much as the next person, but consider how life could unfold if we were to believe that we have enough for what is important. And that we, ourselves, are enough—that we are more than able for the work that is ours to complete.

It is the sense of scarcity (diabolically reinforced by advertising and the media) that makes us think there is not enough to go around. That we have to beat out the next guy. Or that everybody should be equally gifted—which means reducing the entire world to the lowest common denominator.

Even in lean times, what if we considered that we are exactly where we ought to be and that we have enough to be there?

If we assumed that kind of personal accountability, took stock of what we possess, not what we lack, and backed up our actions with a sense of being sufficient to the tasks before us, imagine the challenges we could overcome.

Life has proved to me that as long as I act when guided, stay put when prompted not to take action and engage my Wise Inner Counselor in all aspects of my personal and professional life, I have what I need. No more, no less. Always, exactly, enough.

Reflection 16

GAINING SELF-AWARENESS

*In work and life, what you do not know
can hurt you, especially when that lack
of understanding is about yourself.*

Avoiding Spiritual Bypass

One of life's seeming paradoxes is that many popular approaches to self-awareness do not produce permanent stages of personal development. Without grounding in the physical, we can end up in a state of psychological or spiritual bypass that covers over deep issues of being rather than resolving them. [11]

There are many ways to increase self-awareness. One of the most effective is through mindfulness training.

I once had an opportunity to experience this effectiveness in an all-day awareness workshop during a time when I was dealing with a very stressful family situation. The results changed my life.

A Sensory Awakening

The workshop was being held in a cozy loft furnished with enormous pillows and beanbag chairs that invited relaxation. After introductions, the other participants and I joined in walking barefoot inside and out of doors on various surfaces.

Then, with eyes closed, we handed around objects of many sizes, shapes and textures. We also traced symbols with our fingers, listened to some soothing music, tasted bits of food and breathed in the scent of late spring flowers and aromatic oils.

After the first hour of these activities, which were designed to wake us up mentally and physically, we returned to the loft. Now we were instructed to stand comfortably, close our eyes and take the tiniest step we could possibly execute without falling over.

The purpose was for us to notice every muscle involved in the movement. We were instructed to pay close attention to the feeling of our feet on the carpet and to notice any sounds around us—especially if our body happened to be making them (cracking joints, rumbling tummies, etc.).

Stress Evaporated into Awareness

My mental and emotional stress evaporated as I gave full attention to the subtle movements. As I did so, my awareness of tiny variations became increasingly acute.

The experience was transformational. My body relaxed and fatigue disappeared. I grew joyful and came back to myself in a way I had not been for a very long time. And, better still, a certain cranky, whining voice of negativity went silent.

The workshop was on a Saturday. Throughout Sunday and well into the next week I still had my feet on the ground. Each of my senses continued to tingle with heightened clarity. My heart felt open, compassionately triggering an awareness of some useless habitual behavioral patterns I had never noticed before—which led to further self-discovery.

Give Yourself an Awareness Break

You do not need to engage in a formal workshop to experience the benefits of increasing your awareness. Just go outside.

Take your shoes off and walk with your full attention in the grass or on the beach—or in the rain or snow. Move around your home and really pay attention to the sights and sounds and textures that surround you.

Then take all of that heightened awareness to work with you and observe if you can remain equally engaged, present and mindful. If you have extraordinary experiences, make note of them to remind yourself of the tangible felt sense of being vividly awake in the midst of all your doing.

PART FOUR

Personalizing Great Work

OPENING THE HEART
IN WORK AND LIFE

*What would happen if we actually opened our hearts
to one another on a daily basis—especially at work?*

What Are We Afraid Of?

If I open my heart to your humanity, it follows that I must be open to
my own. Which means I will have to confront not only my joys, but
also my fears—my jealousy, impatience, criticism, irritation and all
the not-so-trivial flaws and foibles of human imperfection.

This can be a frightening proposition.

I also may fear for my reputation. Will I lose my credibility
in the office? Will I be seen as weak or soft or a pushover? What if
people start bringing me all their problems? Will I get overwhelmed
with the drama?

These are real issues in the workplace, especially for those
in executive positions—the ones we may even stereotype as stiff,
starched, self-absorbed and impervious to human needs.

"Isn't that what Human Resources is for?" some may ask—a
comment that causes others to cringe at the idea of reducing to com-
modities the people who are the heart and soul of an organization.

Regardless of what title we give to the personnel function,

if we compartmentalize the heart of an organization into a single department, what will be the experience of every other work group, or even the company's clients and customers?

This is an area that should be of concern to everyone in the organization—and one which those who support managers and executives can actually help them deal with by encouraging an atmosphere of truthful communication.

Great Managers Encourage Open Hearts

I have had the good fortune to work with some truly fantastic managers who brought their open hearts to work with them every day.

They were possessed of what one colleague termed "a kind self-regard" and they extended that kindness to everyone in the company—not only to their department or fellow managers.

They infused their interactions with what another associate called "a feeling of expansive and all-pervading unconditional love so powerful that it affects everything in your experience."

This is not to say they did not go through challenges similar to every other manager. But they did so with such grace and good will that fewer problems arose in their departments than those of their peers.

Merely writing about these three individuals opens my heart and reminds me of how working with them allowed me to feel.

Please notice that I did not say "made me feel."

Their open-heartedness simply facilitated my tapping into my own heart—which is why the memory of those experiences has stayed with me for many years.

I could not help but feel brilliant in their presence. I also felt appreciated, trusted, capable and creative. Those managers saw me as an individual and that vision helped me integrate with positive ways of behaving, prompted by my Wise Inner Counselor.

The key to their success lay in the fact that they were more than cheerleaders or coaches. They were mentors who listened, shared their expertise, made suggestions and delegated according to each employee's abilities.

Their assignments always stretched me and my co-workers while setting us up for success. And on the rare occasions when we did fail, they encouraged us to keep learning and planning for the future success they knew we could achieve.

Invariably, the mentor's message was, "Let me know how I can help." Which meant, "Let me know how I can remove obstacles that might prevent you from doing your best."

How Do You Experience an Open Heart?
Some time ago I posted this question on social media. Here is one particularly inspiring story that I received in response:

> For me an open heart almost always occurs in the service of others. Many years ago I was a young serviceman in uniform and had a chance to assist a mother who had lost her child in a train station. The mother turned to me and asked me to help, trusting in the uniform and the concept of the military as being one of service.
>
> I found the little girl fairly quickly and she very trustingly let me pick her up and take her back to her mother. The trust and the gratitude of the mother, along with the trust and acceptance of my good intentions by the child were amazingly opening to my heart.
>
> That situation taught me that right service to others has many rewards and kicked off a lifetime of seeking to be of help, particularly in public and while on the road.

Qualities of Open-Heartedness
Based on this and other responses to my inquiry, I would like to offer a deeper dive into qualities of someone who is open-hearted:

Positive Flow: Just as the physical heart pumps blood throughout the body, open-heartedness keeps positivity moving, improving the lives of all concerned at work and at home.

Honor: An open-hearted person honors the talents that others bring to life and likewise values his or her own abilities.

Gratitude: Being grateful means having a great attitude toward the opportunities that life offers, even in the form of adversity. The open-hearted person receives all circumstances with equanimity, knowing that gratitude prevents attitudes of entitlement or victimization.

Engagement: The heart's nature is to extend itself, to participate in the matter at hand. Open-hearted people thrive on engaging with others, especially in creative endeavors that help everybody grow.

Relatedness, Not Relationship

I recently gained an important insight: Relationship begins as an activity of relatedness, of connection—a movement of positive thought and feeling between individuals or groups.

However, once a pattern is established, the action can quickly concretize. Unless continually infused with active connection, relationship can morph into a "thing" that we mechanically observe, evaluate or potentially damage through lack of nurturing attention.

Perhaps that is one reason we cherish our pets. They exist in relatedness and their example helps to keep us there.

Knowing When to Act, Or Not

Our Wise Inner Counselor knows when we can take risks, when

we can act, when we should be silent or not act at all. Considering that many situations look alike, the only way to choose a correct response is to engage the inner wisdom that naturally functions through an open heart.

Ultimately, no aspect of relatedness is more important than our openness to receiving the heart's wisdom that comes to us as intuition and discernment.

Here is the birth of compassion that loves unconditionally but is not swayed by the sticky pull of human sympathy that seeks attention, not transformation.

For the wise heart is not a doormat. And the open heart need not close down to protect itself. In the face of situations that may be unsafe or unsuitable, the open heart issues a firm, but loving "No."

My experience in working with and training top performers is that they listen carefully for the subtleties and nuances that make circumstances and people unique. Then they act according to the open heart's intuitive guidance whose direction is unfailingly appropriate to each individual in any given situation.

Reflection 18

Getting to Know Other People

*Have you ever wished you could just
plug in a mind-reading machine and tune
in to what other people are thinking?*

Oh, to Be a Mind-Reader!

My publishing team and I have shared that desire on many occasions—especially when dealing with vendors we have hired for a variety of projects.

We have discovered that knowing our own portion of the process is not sufficient. We must also understand the vendor's part—especially their timelines, internal quality controls and who is responsible for what outcome.

Predictably at first, many vendors are not particularly willing to share the ins and outs of how they conduct their business. Yet when we explain that we are only trying to help them help us, they usually open up and actually become collaborators.

The Power of Inquiry

Absent a real mind-reading machine, the most powerful tool I know of for learning about other people is asking questions. In training circles that approach is called the Socratic Method.

The instructor asks the class questions about a matter being discussed. How the attendees answer the questions reveals more depth and insight than a mere lecture of facts or figures could offer. And because the class provided the answer, they have actually taught themselves.

So if we really want to learn about others, we ask them questions—not from an accusatory or demeaning stance, but from a perspective of genuine curiosity.

Curiosity in Action

One of my colleagues is a gifted salesman. His talent lies in the fact that he is fascinated by other people and he genuinely likes them.

During the time we were both selling books for an independent publishing company, I had the opportunity to watch him in action at a national book fair where our display booth was set up to look like a bookstore.

Rather than sitting in the booth or aggressively hawking books, he would greet people as friends. He would comment on something about them and then ask them a question about their experience at the show. Within less than thirty seconds he would have engaged an individual or group in conversation. He was not telling them about books, he was getting to know them as people.

His interest in them often led them to ask about the books he was promoting. Because he had learned a bit about them, he could recommend some titles he thought they might like and that would do well in their store. He sold a lot of books and, more importantly, people left our booth as partners, not merely as customers.

Showing Genuine Interest in Others

I have seen my salesman friend's process work well in families, self-development retreats and, most dramatically, in the participants of the leadership academy I facilitated.

As soon as they became more aware of the trials and triumphs of their colleagues during the course of a shared meal, they began pulling together as an inspired team.

As dedicated educators and members of a community who wanted to make work and life better for everybody, by the end of the first weekend session of the nine-month program, they had transformed into a solid, self-directed learning group that was dedicated to growing together.

Even simple team-building exercises continued to create strong bonds in unexpected ways—especially between faculty and administrators who had disagreed in the past. Now they were all smiles as they collaborated on practical and innovative solutions to the everyday issues of leadership they all dealt with.

Reflection 19

WHY DON'T WE GET ALONG?

There are many reasons why people do not get along.
One is that they often have conflicting needs.

Sources of Conflict

One of the most challenging projects I ever undertook was to write a three-day course on conflict resolution for the training company I was working for at the time.

I did my best to convince the product development team that I was the last person in the world to write such a course. I had spent most of my life avoiding conflict. I had no experience in mediation and, frankly, working with people who were at each other's throats was the last occupation I would ever have considered.

Nevertheless, managers and fellow instructors (who would have done well to take me at my word) insisted that whatever I wrote would be great. I could have stood up for my intuition that we might all be disappointed with the results, but I didn't.

At least I was true to my own principles. I finally acquiesced on the condition that I be allowed to create a course for individuals and groups who actually wanted to resolve their conflicts.

Not surprisingly, those persons did not attend my course. They were already resolving their conflicts through self-observation, dialogue and collaboration. The individuals who were usually sent to this course tended to be those who provoked conflicts and who firmly believed that everyone but themselves was to blame.

After teaching a couple of disastrous on-site courses in which managers who were often the main source of conflict came in late, refused to participate in discussions and learning exercises, left early and then pulled others out of class, I turned the course over to instructors who relished dealing with trouble-makers.

What I Learned

Despite the stress and disappointment that my inside-out approach did not actually resolve issues of dealing with truly fractious people, I learned a lot about why folks do not get along.

I studied a number of methods for resolving conflict and finally turned to Maslow's Hierarchy of Human Needs[12] for his clear observations into why individuals and groups working in the same company on the same projects can have trouble finding common ground.

Maslow's answer is that they may have different needs, which range from foundational matters of safety and survival to what he termed "Being" needs of self-actualization and self-transcendence.

A Fictional Scenario About Getting Along

As a way to enhance the learning experience for course participants, the production team at my company decided that we should create videos to demonstrate a group of co-workers who were functioning at the various levels of Maslow's hierarchy of needs.

That worked well for an in-person course. For the purposes of this book, I would like to tell you a fictitious story I wrote about what could happen to a talented team that is having trouble getting along because of their conflicting needs.

THE CHALLENGE OF CONFLICTING NEEDS

Maslow would have identified the members of this very competent team as self-actualizers because of how they are able to use their natural talents. They are normally highly productive, which is important because they are working on a major initiative for their organization.

Unfortunately, through a variety of circumstances, in recent weeks they each have faced challenges to their personal well-being and professional effectiveness.

Until these situations are resolved, the atmosphere in their office will likely become more intense. They may find themselves believing that others on their team are directly or indirectly blocking them from getting what they need in order to return to the high level of professionalism they expect of themselves and each other.

The Cast of Characters

Jeff is the only married member of the team. His wife recently had a baby who confuses nighttime with playtime. Jeff's perspective on work and life has been effectively reduced to his desperate need for sleep.

Sally lives in a neighborhood in which several break-ins have occurred. She feels unsafe and anxious, which is making her less efficient in the office.

In addition, she feels overwhelmed by her workload and believes that her supervisor, Delores, is singling her out for criticism.

Fred was recently hired as executive assistant to Delores. Most of the other executive assistants in the company are women who have their own social cliques.

Fred does not know where he fits in the organization's social structure, and members of his own team are so preoccupied with their own problems that they have not reached out to him.

Clive feels that he has outgrown his job. He has been taking some self-development courses, and his life coach is encouraging him to seek other work that is more in line with his natural talents.

He suspects that his co-workers resent his insistence on advancement because they were all working toward similar goals. Until Clive finds a new job that is better suited to his need to actualize his potential abilities, he may have trouble keeping his harmony.

Delores is hoping for a promotion based on her team's completion of their big project. She has worked hard for advancement and will be devastated if she does not get the recognition she believes she deserves.

As supervisor, Delores is pivotal to resolving her team's troubles. But first she must address her own need for external approval.

Until she decides that the success or failure of her team does not determine her worth as a person, she cannot help her co-workers get their needs met and put their considerable talents back to work. Fortunately, she receives help at the right time.

Help Arrives

Members of Delores's team have complained about what they perceive as their supervisor's failures as a manager to **Gerry**, the head of Human Resources, which she calls the Personnel Effectiveness Department.

Gerry's training, experience and reliance on her own

inner guidance suggest that the underlying challenge for this team is lack of communication. She decides to take a proactive approach and invites Delores to her office to discuss the matter.

Gerry's Meeting with Delores

"They've been complaining, haven't they?" demanded Delores the minute she entered Gerry's office and sat down heavily across from her.

"Well, I have some complaints of my own. If this team doesn't start pulling their weight, we'll never meet our deadlines. I feel like I'm the only one who does any real work around here."

Gerry took a deep breath and smiled at Delores.

"Before we get into who is or is not pulling their weight, I would like to hear about what your team *has* accomplished. I know you've been working very hard and I'd appreciate a progress report."

Gerry's non-confrontational tone caught Delores's attention and she also took a deep breath. She pulled out a spreadsheet that detailed her team's progress. Beside each task that was completed or under way was the name of the person who was handling that part of the project.

While Delores explained each section of the spread-sheet, she occasionally looked up. The expression on her face showed how urgently she wanted Gerry to congrat-ulate her on all of the work that actually had been accom-plished despite the team's personal challenges. However, the other woman merely indicated that she understood.

"Well?" said Delores when she had finished. She tried to hold back her exasperation, but was not entirely successful.

"Well," answered Gerry in an even tone, "I could give

you my opinion, but I would like to hear your assessment of what you have presented to me."

Delores looked surprised. As she had gone through the report, being forced to deal with facts caused her to reevaluate her statement that members of her team were not pulling their weight.

Clearly, she was not the only one who was moving the project forward, although she was correct that she had been working very hard to make up for some delays.

"I guess we're not as far behind as I thought," said Delores rather sheepishly. "In fact, if I looked at this report from the outside, I would have to say this is a very dedicated group."

"What would you say about their supervisor?" asked Gerry with a twinkle in her eye.

"I would say that overall she was doing a pretty good job." Delores teared up when she said this. She was so hard on herself that this admission was new to her.

"But then why are they complaining?" she asked, genuinely bewildered.

"Why do you think?" countered Gerry kindly.

Delores thought a minute. "Well, it could be that we don't talk to each other. I mean, we discuss details of the project, but there is no real team spirit. Is that my fault?"

"These things happen sometimes when other issues are troubling even our most talented people," Gerry explained. "I'd like to suggest that you have a team meeting away from the office and let's see if we can put the sparkle back into this group."

Delores nodded, but looked doubtful.

"Would you like for me to facilitate the discussion?" Gerry offered.

"Oh, I really would," said Delores. Her expression

brightened, but then she frowned. "Do you think they'll want to talk to me?"

"I'm sure of it," said Gerry. "I believe they will be very grateful to share the challenges they haven't told you about. And I have a feeling some excellent solutions will emerge rather quickly."

Commentary

Although this scenario is a bit of fiction, the situation is potentially very real—as is the solution.

If we were to follow Gerry, Delores and the others through their off-site meeting, we would observe that inviting each person to share their concerns and burdens created an atmosphere of mutual understanding and compassion for the challenges they each were facing.

Such potential confrontations as this team faced in their meeting do require a skilled facilitator, which Gerry happened to be. By the end of the discussion, everyone had relaxed and was surprised at how easily their needs could be met with everyone working together.

Meeting Outcomes

Jeff was given the opportunity to work flexible hours until his baby started sleeping through the night so he could catch up on his own rest. **Fred** generously offered to help Jeff finish some of his reports which were coming due very soon.

Sally worked out her differences regarding her workload with **Delores**, and **Clive** suggested a safer neighborhood where there was an apartment for rent that Sally could afford. **Everyone** volunteered to help her move.

As a result of **Fred's** being able to express his concern that he didn't know where he fit, his co-workers let him know that they considered him a vital team member and promised to include him in more group project planning discussions and social events.

Delores gained much valuable insight into her team and her actual effectiveness as their supervisor. She began to experience an inner shift toward a resilient self-esteem rather than depending on the approval of others for her sense of worthiness.[13]

Finally, at **Gerry's** suggestion, **Clive** was put in charge of a new aspect of the team project, which opened up possibilities he had not been aware of and which were aligned with some of the career advancement issues he had been struggling with.

Commentary on Gerry's Facilitation Skills

In her own work, Gerry consistently relied on her Wise Inner Counselor for insight into the many difficult situations that present themselves to anyone who deals with an organization's people issues.

After the team members had all shared the stories of their concerns and burdens, she invited them to turn their attention to their own inner guidance to help resolve future challenges.

This was an approach that surprised them at first.

However, as Gerry suspected—because she knew quite a bit about their true capabilities—they welcomed the suggestion and appreciated her trust in their ability to tap into rich personal sources of intuition.

Team Building Takes Time

Complete transformation of the team was not instantaneous. Old patterns die hard. But everyone agreed to stay open to conversation and innovative ways in which they could each help the team realize its potential as a high-functioning group of self-actualizers.

Some weeks later, when they had successfully completed their project, they were all quite surprised that Delores did not receive the promotion she had wanted.

However, by that time she had decided it made no difference to her. She was working with a great team and she wanted to keep them together.

They all heartily agreed.

Reflection 20

EMBRACING THE PERSONAL IN PROCESS

"Enjoy the process!" a wise mentor used to remind me.
"Take time to get involved and enjoy the camaraderie."

A Journey, Not a Destination

If you are a "make-it-happen" kind of person, you may be more focused on checking off items from your "To-Do" lists than on the actual process of getting to completion.

Finishers are a rare breed and are much-appreciated by their organizations. But do you have fun on the way to the finish line? Do you actually enjoy the personal aspects of reaching your goals?

Like life, work is a journey, not a destination. And top performers who thrive embrace the possibilities, even the rough roads, taking them all in stride while finding the joy in the experience.

Humor Opens Minds and Hearts

My fellow instructors and I used to joke that we were in the "edu-tainment" business. It was absolutely essential that we and our students enjoy the course—especially because people-skills training often asks attendees to change behaviors, even self-concepts. And that can be challenging.

However, when people are laughing, the process is easier. This was never clearer to me than when I helped write and teach a new course on assertiveness skills.

Most of the attendees were more reticent types who had been sent to the course by bosses who apparently thought everyone should play hardball at the office.

These poor souls had arrived very worried that they were going to be subjected to some kind of boot camp experience. When I explained that we would be exploring effective assertiveness—which had nothing to do with bullying—they relaxed.

The author of this course was an exceptional facilitator who understood the power of humor. So to teach the various techniques, we created fake soap opera scenarios for groups of three to role-play, practicing the technique being highlighted.

The course materials provided the soap opera scenarios, but it was up to their small groups to figure out the scene and then present it to the class. The results were truly incredible.

Never in my life have I witnessed such transformation. The role-plays they created were hysterically funny and right on target. Even the shyest students got into the act.

No More Limp-Fish Handshakes

At the end of the course, individuals who had barely shaken my hand on the first morning now stood before their classmates to declare that when people met them in the future, they would be greeted by a confident smile and a firm grip.

No more doormats. No more limp-fish handshakes. No more looking away when confronted by an aggressive person. The energy of laughter moving in and around the class had given them—some for the first time—the tangible experience of standing tall, speaking up and reaching out.

Teaching this course provided me one of the most profound lessons I ever learned about working with people. The tears that filled my eyes on the last day were stirred from my being deeply touched by the sparkle that now shown out from faces that had come to class looking very apprehensive.

Communication Is Vital for Process

If I had to identify the single biggest challenge that arose for my business students and colleagues, it would be communication. We simply do not know how to talk to each other.

We do not speak the same language as those around us. Departments and industries often develop their own lingo that has evolved from specialized functions or from a desire to exclude those not of their "tribe." Sometimes I think we purposefully emphasize the differences.

I remember how we proudly displayed our "Video Spoken Here" buttons in my television production days. This exclusivity did not encourage friendly relations with other departments who needed our services. I am sorry to recall that we liked it that way.

Connecting with Your Audience

Anyone who has ever given a presentation hoping to elicit a positive response knows that you must tailor your message to the audience. Not only do departments and industries use unique words, but the style in which they prefer to deliver and receive information is also unique.

Here are just a few examples of different audience preferences—some of which I learned the hard way when teaching people skills to very diverse groups:

> **Groups with a preference for analytical thinking** tended to speak clearly and concisely, and they wanted me to do the same. They preferred being presented with facts and few frills. They wanted to see costs up front and proof of how they were calculated.

The presentation had to make rational and economic sense—and I had to be able to answer their questions pertaining to the bottom line.

Groups with strong organizational preferences were more attentive to a sequential presentation with clear bullet points illustrating the details of the material.

I always made sure to check my slides and handouts for typos and my clothes for wrinkles. I arrived early and finished on time because they valued punctuality.

Groups who were especially people-oriented tended to enjoy stories about how the course would enhance their quality of life and that of their clients. It was important that they experienced a personal connection with me and that they felt I understood their concerns.

Groups who focused on the big picture considered the medium as the message. They preferred course materials that were visually rich and uniquely compelling.

The exercises they liked best were short and entertaining. These folks were easily bored, but they immediately perked up when presented with an innovation that challenged them to stretch their personal limits.[14]

Covering All Your Bases

I quickly learned to include something for everyone in my presentations because, just as soon as I thought I had a group figured out, they would surprise me with an unexpected response—like the baseball batter who just bunted when you thought he was going to swing.

Reflection 21

THE POWER OF STORY
TO PERSONALIZE

*Our brains are wired for story. It seems that
we must have story in our lives or perish.*

Stories Reinforce Our Humanity

One reason that small business is the backbone of many local economies is the fact that each of these ventures is a social as well as a financial activity, started by people to support themselves and to meet certain necessities of other people in their community.

The question becomes how to enhance those social connections in, around and through a business. The use of real-life stories is one very powerful answer.

Storytelling is currently a popular marketing tool. It is also one of the oldest forms of communication. Our brains are actually wired for story, and it seems that we must have story or perish.

Acknowledging our mutual humanity through sharing our stories creates remarkable connection. Group facilitators know that one of the most effective ways to encourage interaction is to ask individuals to tell the group something about themselves.

Everyone has a story!

In the telling, everybody in the group discovers that "your

story is also my story." The challenges we face as human beings are often more similar than different. As we accept each other for the foibles we describe, we naturally relax any self-criticism because we can so easily relate to one another's situations and how each of us responds to them.

Storytelling Can Heal

Telling your story to a stranger during cross-country travel used to be a time-honored tradition. The practice can have a healing effect. The one who tells the story has the opportunity to review her life without judgment from another person. And the stranger easily extends a compassionate ear because she has not been involved in the other person's history.

At the end of the story, they go their separate ways, but they are strangers no longer. Now they are fellow travelers in the vast social network of humanity. And they each know more about themselves than they did before their stories brought them together.

Storytelling at the End of Life

I discovered another practical example of the healing power of story while presenting public education workshops for The Denver Hospice. Both medical and non-medical personnel told me how important it is for those nearing death to recount their experiences in this life.

Often, as they relate their personal history to a loved one or hospice worker, they come to a realization of their life's value— almost as if telling the story serves as a sort of confessional in which they forgive themselves for any real or imagined mistakes.

I observed this exact phenomenon with my elderly mother. Several years before her passing at age 94, I suggested that she write her memoirs. "Oh, I haven't had a very interesting life," she protested. "Well, then why don't you write me a letter about some of your memories," I suggested.

Sixty-four double-sided pages later, written in her precise longhand, she realized that she had lived an amazing life, especially for someone who had grown up in the Missouri Ozarks during the Depression of the 1930s.

She and my father had lived all over the United States. She had witnessed history being made during and after the years of World War II as the world changed at break-neck speed. She had traveled to Europe, met fascinating people and learned to bloom where she was planted. We both agreed that hers was a life well lived.

Stories Make Business Social

One of the most exciting projects I worked on while producing a PBS Business Channel television series was at a conference called "Storytelling & Business Excellence" held at the International Storytelling Institute in historic Jonesborough, Tennessee.

In attendance were executives from companies as diverse as World Bank, Disney Imagineering, Pillsbury, Capitol One, Shell Oil and Eastman Chemical.

These leaders had assembled to share ways in which their companies were using story to build dynamic corporate cultures and highly effective knowledge management systems.

Some years before the conference, World Bank had decided to become a knowledge sharing organization rather than a strictly financial institution. The senior executive charged with facilitating the change had been trying to make his point to colleagues with standard flip charts and PowerPoint presentations.

They showed very little interest in his proposals until he told them the story of a villager in Africa who had received a laptop computer from World Bank.

During an outbreak of malaria in his village, the young African had dialed into the CDC web site and found information on how to treat malaria. He took the information back to his village and stopped the outbreak.

Because that story dealt with real people, it turned an abstract idea of sharing knowledge into a tangible, palpable concept with emotional impact. And it moved the executive's colleagues into action.

The representative of Disney Imagineering (the organization that designs theme parks and creates new rides and experiences) reported that they regularly consulted with Disney elders to determine if they were continuing to innovate in a manner consistent with Disney values, culture and heritage.

At the time of the storytelling conference, the oldest employee was in his 90s and still reported to an actual (not honorary) job. He had been with Disney for sixty years and literally embodied their heritage, having worked directly with the founders, Walt and Roy. Younger employees and managers sought him out for his wisdom and honored him as an icon.

The Disney executive explained: "We're in the story business. We understand the importance of keeping our stories alive, passing them on from generation to generation, in new employee orientation, training and development. We live our culture through our stories."

And, of course, as individuals depart and others arrive to take their place, the stories inevitably change. For better or for worse, the culture changes with them.

What Storytellers Know

Traditional storytellers will tell you that stories die if they are not told and retold. They see the connection between a healthy society and the strength of its oral heritage. They also say that story is as essential to human life as air and water. In the absence of positive story, negative story will appear.

The real power in an organization lies with the storytellers. If you want to change a company culture, you must first change the story that people tell each other about how they work together, what is important to them, what they know about their collective history and what they expect from their future.

Organizations and communities are built on a shared vision that engages the passion, imagination and commitment of people. Wise leaders understand that storytelling is the best way to communicate that vision.

If the narrative is compelling, others will catch the message and make it their own. Once that happens, they will naturally continue telling the story, making it richer with each recitation, which attracts more people to the vision.

The Stories We Tell Ourselves

If this is the way storytelling operates, we might well ask, "What story is my organization or community telling itself? Is it positive or negative? Who are the storytellers and what is their perspective?"

We may also ask ourselves, "What is my internal narrative? What do I say to and about myself when no one else is around?"

Here is a vital role played by our Wise Inner Counselor, who speaks to us and about us only in Love. The tale of our inherent truth, beauty and goodness is the story our True Self would have us repeat.

Reflection 22

Overcoming the Shadow in Work and Life

Dealing with the false self is a challenge. Fortunately, the life force trapped in negative patterns wants to be liberated.

When Darkness Comes to Light

Have you ever felt that almost as soon as you choose to honor your values and act with integrity, every possible doubt, fear, annoyance or distraction arises to thwart your determination to be more balanced in all your doing? That is your shadow (the not-self, also called the false or synthetic self) coming into the light to be liberated.

The Shadow Lives Underground

The shadow consists of all those disowned, discarded or suppressed elements of our psyche that lie beneath the surface of awareness, waiting to trip us up.

Like the proverbial devil on our shoulder, they prompt us to do and say exactly what we did not intend. They run those unconscious scripts of fear and negativity that keep us trapped in ways of thinking, feeling and behaving that are not useful.

These are the patterns in others that probably rub us the wrong way. And they likely are the repetitious behaviors we exhibit that trigger negative responses from our colleagues and loved ones.

When Wounded Inner Children Appear at Work

One of the reasons I left corporate training was my realization that many so-called business or performance issues were really matters of unresolved personal psychology.

Our workplaces do tend to operate like families—sometimes highly dysfunctional ones. We get to resolve our parental issues with authority figures. Co-workers substitute for siblings. And if we are supervisors, we may find ourselves surrounded by unruly adult children. So what should we do when they are having tantrums and generally behaving badly?

Effective Assertiveness to the Rescue

According to the course I taught, assertiveness is first and foremost the right for each of us to be true to our self, but not at the expense of others. Being assertive is not license to insult, berate or subjugate. It is the freedom to explore our personal motivations, values and principles, and to actualize our goals, dreams and inspirations.

The secret to being effectively assertive lies in knowing what we want and asking for it. But that "what we want" must be based on the deeply held core values of our True Self. [15]

A Test of Core Values

Our decision to assertively stand up for our values may be tested at any time. As it happened, my principle of protecting the integrity of the classroom was sorely tried while teaching this very course.

The class was on a break after the first morning session—which was critical to creating a setting in which the participants, many of whom were very shy, would feel safe to step far outside their comfort zone to practice being assertive.

I was preparing to take my own break when a large man barged into the classroom. Very aggressively, he said he had won a free course and he was going to take this one.

I am not a tall person, but I am an assertive one. I politely, but firmly, replied that he was welcome to take the course another time. However, I was not going to admit him because he had missed the essential set-up for the two-day course. This made him angry.

I knew the company would support my decision, because maintaining a safe environment in the classroom was one of their core values. So I walked the man to the front desk and told the ed center director why I was not admitting him to my class. (What I did not say was that inner guidance clearly warned me about him.)

Even when the man became verbally abusive and actually threw a tantrum, I stood my ground. He eventually left, vowing to have me fired. Of course, I called headquarters myself to report the incident. They did support me, and I never heard any more about it.

Who Do You Think You Are?

Actions flow from beliefs, and the most important beliefs are the ones we hold about ourselves. We treat ourselves according to our self-image. And because we see the world as we are, not as it is, we also view others through that lens.

If I believe myself to be weak, ignorant, unimportant and beholden to authoritative or abusive people, I will likely act the part—giving up my power and influence to those I perceive as stronger or more worthy, inviting them to treat me with disrespect.

However, if I see myself as my Wise Inner Counselor does, I will champion my soul's integrity. I will also help others stand up for their highest principles and fulfill their own innate potential.

Self-Observation Is Vital

Most of our negative behaviors are unintended and unconscious. Unfortunately, these patterns kick in automatically before we can make a conscious choice about an alternate response.

We must learn to take a time out, to catch ourselves in the

act—actually before the act. Then we have a very good chance of following our better intentions, rather than letting our wounded inner child throw a tantrum.

The ability to control the mind and emotions through self-observation is one of the most powerful abilities which we humans possess. We may walk around in a unconscious state much of the time. But if we choose, we can change that behavior by engaging the Wise Inner Counselor as an inner witness so we become conscious of our automatic responses.

We usually experience a subtle energy shift before one of these scripts runs. If we can become aware of that energetic change, we can disrupt the autopilot and start making effective choices. Asking a therapist or counselor to help us identify those ego structures of which we are not consciously aware can also be useful.

Ego Wants to Participate in its Own Liberation

One of the most profound concepts I have learned from studying a variety of personal growth models is that the positive life force trapped in the wounded self's identity structure actually wants to participate in its own liberation.

Many of the ego's defensive patterns were formed when we were very young as the best way we knew at the time for dealing with an overwhelming environment. This often meant stifling huge chunks of our true nature.

As we mature psychologically, those limiting ego patterns are no longer necessary or useful. We begin to realize that it is time to relieve them of the duty they assumed when we were children.

Regardless of what practices we use for self-observation, our goal is to become more aligned with our True Self by loving back into awareness those aspects of identity that have gone unloved for a very long time. As I have learned to catch myself before the automatic response kicks in, I have become better able to remain flexible in all aspects of my life as circumstances change. Which they will.

PART FIVE

Doing Your Great Work

in a Changing World

Reflection 23

ADAPTABILITY IS
A GREAT IDEA

*Change is inevitable. How we choose to
adapt to the shifts makes all the difference.*

Remaining Relevant

Markets change. Society's priorities and values change. If we want to stay relevant and engaged in creating a better world, we must remain conversant with lessons of the past and grounded in realities of the present as we open our minds and hearts to the possibilities of a future that will not wait for us to catch up.

More Than Letting Go of the Past

I learned from the re-engineering expert whose assistant I was that every industry has a life cycle. So do organizations and careers. Which means we must be prepared to reinvigorate our companies, our departments and ourselves if we are to continue to flourish.

This realization and a willingness to release the past is vital. However, in being flexible we do not simply let go. We sense a new direction. We envision a better future. We strategize. We plan. And we create—all of which takes courage.[16]

Volatile times encourage us to embrace change as an opportunity to evolve to a higher consciousness. In fact, we ourselves may become agents of change because we foresee the future. And we desire to shape it because we are not content with the status quo or former successes.

We understand that the greatest threat to our future success is where we have excelled in the past. We do not wait for obsolescence to creep in. We recognize and seize new opportunities. And if we do not see them, we create them.

Tilling the Soil

As a performer, writer and instructor, I know well that creativity is the process that shakes disparate pieces together—ideally fashioning something more useful, more beautiful and more transcendent than what previously existed.

If you have ever done any home remodeling, you also know that some purposeful destruction is part of the process—which doesn't make the creative demolition any less unsettling, even if you had previously welcomed the changes.

I think we should call the process tilling the soil for new seeds to be planted. That is more in keeping with creativity's intention.

Clear Vision Guides Productive Creativity

Having a vision of what you plan to create makes all the difference. I am reminded of my husband's delight in tearing out half a wall, old carpet and tile in preparation for the stunning oak floors and natural cherry wood fireplace surround he was hand-crafting for the living room in our town home.

I could not see the design he held in his mind's eye, so the dramatic changes were a challenge for me. Fortunately, as he completed this and other professional-grade woodworking projects, I learned to trust his vision because he made it a reality for me.

This was an important lesson because I knew that Stephen often took bold actions based on inspiration from his Wise Inner

Counselor. Eventually, I had to laugh at my initial reaction to the renovations he was making in our home environment because I had been taking similarly bold actions for most of my life.

Mine did not usually involve such physical alterations, but the overall effect of creative change in my life was the same.

Where Do Those Dramatic Ideas Originate?

My sense is that our best ideas are spiritually inspired. Even more vital than restructuring our outer environment is the process of remodeling the inner one.

Our greatest work may be transforming and transcending our former self. For that project, the Wise Inner Counselor acts as the general contractor who ensures that we are following our soul's original blueprint.

Creating a Synthesis of Marvelous Newness

New ideas may appear as a package containing the vision of an entire solution that can be elaborated and implemented.

Ideas often come to us whole—perhaps with a bit of fanfare—that rush of energy that accompanies *a-ha!* They can sail in, seemingly from afar, landing in the heart and mind with a joyful "plunk" that takes us by surprise, even when we have worked hard to be original in our thinking.

We are frequently surprised at the suddenness of the arrival of these new ideas and at the pure elegance of their applicability, effectiveness and simplicity. So we honor our creative process and try our best to stay out of its way.

Oh, yes, we do our homework—often long, deliberate hours of it. And while we are doing our part of the process, we trust that truly unique solutions will emerge from the mystery of well-schooled intuition and the creative energy that twists, turns and tumbles bits of information into a synthesis of marvelous newness.

Knowing What to Prune

How do we know what to keep and what to eliminate? This is where we rely again on courage and the wisdom of the heart—the seat of the Wise Inner Counselor. It is our balanced outer awareness, attuned to our internal soul compass, that wisely informs the moment of choice.

Keeping in mind that adaptability does not mean instability, capriciousness or change for its own sake, we prune only when certain elements have shown themselves to be obsolete or worn out. Then we make the courageous decision and move forward.

Achieving a Higher Purpose

Being adaptable also means having a sense of the upward flow of cultural evolution. Moving in consonance with that flow, we aim to achieve a higher purpose for individuals and organizations.

Very often that purpose is the fulfillment of a personal or group mission or goal. And here is another essential element of adaptability—being mission-driven and goal-oriented.

We alter our direction when the old processes no longer move us closer to our goals—or when the goals change altogether. And we always do our best to create strategically, based on best practices and core principles.

Bringing an innovative solution into existence is one of the most rewarding aspects of adaptability. When we allow the new to include and then transcend what came before, the exhilaration of a job well done can encourage us to take on and complete even greater challenges in the future.

ADAPTING TO COMPLETION

*How do we approach endings with
kindness? One answer lies in focusing
on completion rather than closure.*

Loss Happens

As much as we try to avoid them, losses occur at home and at work. Loved ones or cherished pets may pass away. Jobs may be lost to downsizing or closures. Natural disasters may strike entire communities, creating enormous financial and emotional losses.

Industries may be forced to make radical changes to stay current with the shifting demands of a world streaking toward an unknown and often frightening future.

Positive Changes Require Flexibility

Positive changes also require flexibility of body, mind and spirit. Welcome events such as marriages, promotions, new babies, new homes, graduations and retirements all challenge us to adapt.

Positive change brings with it a sense of loss for our previous status—perhaps as a single person, a couple with a happily noisy brood of teenagers or a productively employed worker. The same event can have different meanings for different people.

I remember speaking about change to a service club's breakfast meeting. Most of the members were retirement age and some were a few years older.

One of the recent retirees sheepishly admitted to the group, "Yeah, now that I'm retired I spend a lot more time at home. And my wife spends a lot of time away from home playing bridge. We didn't expect the change to be difficult, but it is."

Everybody laughed because they had all been through similar experiences.

Reaching a Goal Is a Type of Loss

A consultant friend of mine often coaches entrepreneurs to help them process an unanticipated grief when they successfully sell a company or a product they have worked hard to bring to market.

They may have met an important goal, and yet releasing their creation to others can feel a bit like sending their child off to the first day of kindergarten. If they do not acknowledge their mixed feelings, those emotions can block their ability to fully commit to their next project or innovation.[17]

A Process, Not a Mandate

For several years I wrote and conducted workshops and retreats on end-of-life and grief issues.

What struck me most profoundly during those events was the concept of "letting go"—and how we may inadvertently use it to wound ourselves or others. The rush to move on can make the grief of loss worse than it already is.

Once I was helping with registration at a reunion picnic for people who had served at a non-profit organization where I had also worked. One of the attendees was a lady whose husband had recently passed away. When I offered to give her a hug, she burst into tears and then immediately apologized.

"Oh, I'm sorry to be such a mess," she sobbed. "My sister said

I should let him go and move on. But I just can't. I feel like such a failure."

The poor woman had not even held her husband's memorial service and already her sister was berating her for not moving on. My heart went out to her as I explained that letting go is a process, not a mandate.

I assured her that she would know when she was ready to move forward—as life called her—not as she forced herself to meet her own or others' expectations of how she should respond to this devastating loss.

We Have Forgotten That Loss Is Natural

One reason we may try to rush through the inevitable grief which accompanies any loss is that the pain is foreign to us. Our technological world has so removed us from many natural life processes that we are likely to experience grief as random, unsettlingly mysterious and primal in its ability to overwhelm us.

Although society is changing its approach to life's beginnings, we still try to shield ourselves from the pain of its endings. Our challenge is to realize that life is a continual progression of beginnings and endings.

If we are afraid to embrace an ending, we may find it more difficult to begin anew because the energy we need to move forward is tied up in looking back.

Remaining Open to Process Feelings

We speak of wanting closure after experiencing a profound loss. We just want the suffering to stop—which is understandable. But there are lessons in that pain and resolution to be discovered at the bottom of grief's dark well of emotion, if we will let it do its work.

During my own grieving process after my husband died, I learned that as long as I was striving to integrate the essence of our experience into my own being, deep emotions and expectations had a way of letting go of me when they were complete. For me, the integration process included a lot of storytelling—in person with friends and in print in the memoir I was writing. [18]

Stories Can Bring Completion

Multiple experiences have shown me that one of the reasons we are compelled to tell the stories of our loss, remembering an event or a loved one, is that with each telling we internalize a bit more of that experience. Eventually we begin to notice its presence in us rather than its absence from us.

This process is just as important at work as it is at home. Perhaps more so, because there are so many task-related demands on our attention that we may not take time to process deep emotions.

However, when we adopt a mindset of celebrating completions, we inevitably discover that as individuals and work groups we are much more adaptable to changes, both small and large.

Completion Dissolves Limitations

Here are a few patterns, attitudes and concepts that can release our energy for new beginnings when we allow them to come to completion rather than hanging on to them or berating ourselves that we should be letting them go before we are ready:

Failures: Losing face, money, time or credibility because a project failed is tough. But what did we learn?

When I ask workshop participants to identify their most significant life lessons, they often speak of an apparent failure that led to important insights. When we find and embrace the lesson, the experience is complete.

Successes: Celebrate achievements. We tell stories of how our team transcended what we thought we could do. We acknowledge our collective accomplishments and then set our sights on what comes next—knowing that future success will not look like the past.

Victimization: Eleanor Roosevelt famously said, "No one can make you feel inferior without your consent."[19]

When we focus on criticism or negative projections from others, we lose sight of our own actions that form the foundation for the great work we hope to perform.

Gratitude: The surest remedy I know for turning victimization on its head is to start expressing everything in your life—past or present—for which you are grateful.

This can be a challenging exercise for individuals or groups who are determined to perpetuate sour concepts of themselves or others, but it works.

Fresh Perceptions Bring New Beginnings

When I was teaching creative problem solving, one of the tips I liked to share was the idea of stimulating new perceptions throughout the day.

One creativity expert I cited said that for over ten years he deliberately took different, often circuitous routes to his office. Without fail, when he got to work, assumptions and preconceptions of his current project had disappeared.

Bending in the Wind

The ability to remain flexible as circumstances move forward from beginnings to completions and then on to new beginnings can be one of life's most liberating experiences.

As we realize that life continues to unfold in self-renewing spirals of growth and more refined consciousness, the better able are we to help others do the same—which is a very effective way to make a positive difference in the world.

Reflection 25

BEING NATURALLY AUTHENTIC

The more we develop a kind and compassionate self-regard, the more we simply stop pretending to be other than who or what we really are.

Stretching into New Possibilities

Like my riding instructor's lesson horses when she turns them out to go running unbridled in the fields by her arena, we long to run free in our true nature. When we have liberated ourselves from limiting perceptions of ourselves, that freedom is a real possibility.

Life does not always offer the opportunity for employment in areas of our preference, which can be a good thing. Working outside of our comfort zone stretches us, widens our perspective and deepens our knowledge about ourselves and the world we inhabit.

We may also discover areas of interest that eventually call us to unusual occupations that feel perfectly natural, although we might never have considered them.

Detecting an Inner Calling

My colleagues have confirmed for me the importance of identifying where we have been and what we were doing when we were most in tune with our Wise Inner Counselor.

Moments of profound connection with inner guidance can occur at any time, anywhere. The occasion really does not matter. What is important is the tangible, felt sense that we have struck gold in one of those *a-ha!* moments which proclaim we have detected a calling that is genuinely ours.

My *Eureka!* Moment

Some years ago I accompanied the management consultant I was assisting to a meeting with a select marketing group that was planning a series of seminars to offer as a value-added service for their clients.

As soon as they began describing their course materials, I could barely stop myself from leaping out of my chair and begging them for a job. On the inside I was shouting, "I want to do seminars!"

My heart was racing. I felt like dancing. The whole room seemed lit up with my enthusiasm for an occupation I had never considered until that moment.

Although my background was in theater and I had done a bit of lecturing, I had never really considered becoming an instructor. But there it was—a calling—an undeniable stirring in my very soul.

Eventually, I did become a business training instructor where I discovered sides of myself I had never been challenged to explore. I loved those challenges because the real requirement for success was for me to become more genuinely my True Self.

I sincerely wanted to help the attendees get the most from the courses I was teaching. The only way that was going to happen was for me to be emotionally balanced, focused in the present moment and as honest with myself as I wanted to be with my audience.

Motivated by the Desire to Serve

Many of my fellow instructors recognize their desire to serve their students as a prime motivator for them to become grounded in their own authenticity.

When I asked them about their strongest motivations, they offered these comments:

- Whether the audience is less than a dozen or fills a lecture hall, my experience is the same. As soon as I put my attention on the fact that people are on their way, I feel my heart opening to welcome them.

- I become very curious about where they are from, why they have decided on this course, what they hope to gain from attending, challenges they are facing.

- As the presentation progresses, I notice that as I allow myself to be vulnerable—admitting when I do not have all the answers or sharing a difficult experience—the more readily the attendees volunteer to share their own experiences and insights. Everybody benefits.

- I feel very comfortable in my own skin. Fresh insights pop into my awareness as my intuition becomes heightened. Ideas flow freely and the easy humor that I consider a hallmark of my personal style appears as well.

- I am more in tune with my body than usual because I am paying acute attention to everything that is occurring in the room—including my own kinesthetic responses.

- I feel a deep connection with the people in the classroom. In fact, at some point in our shared learning experience, I start seeing them as souls who possess an inner light.

- A higher power takes over. I become aware of being a vehicle for profound wisdom to be present in the room. I am not so much doing the presenting as I am being incorporated into a transcendent experience that inspires everybody in the class—myself included.

When Being Real Becomes Transcendent

Full engagement can precipitate that magical moment when craft becomes art. And we need not be artists to have the experience.

We learn and practice hard, doing what it takes to internalize the details of our occupation until they become second nature. Then, at some point in the midst of being deeply engaged in our work, we let go of the details—releasing them into that sublime moment when all effort falls away.

For then we are simply being the dance or the painting or the time-saving innovation or the perfectly executed business presentation. We become the music of what's happening and the experience feels absolutely natural.

The Mickey Dunne Group, traditional Irish musicians whose natural artistry is truly magical. *Photo courtesy of Amba Gale.*

Reflection 26

LEARNING AND LEADING AS LIFELONG PURSUITS

Learning and leading are inextricably linked. Our
very presence teaches others what we have become.
We are always leading—if only by example.

What Does It Mean to Lead?

True leaders are the vanguard. They go first. They learn the best route to the desired destination.

Only then do they lead their followers through the mountain passes, over the rivers, around the brambles and under dangerous overhangs to arrive safely at the end of a journey that individuals alone would be hard-pressed to complete.

Yet, as the ancient philosopher Lao Tzu observed, "A leader is best when people barely know he exists. When his work is done, his aim fulfilled, they will say: 'We did it ourselves'." [20]

Our world is in the throes of competing approaches to leadership. Regardless of what type prevails, we will always need leaders who are also mentors. If you have ever served on a large committee, you know this to be true. Someone must help guide the proceedings and facilitate the group's coming to effective conclusions.

Creating Mutual Resonance

Whom do we trust to lead us safely through the perils of present circumstances, to bring our project safely to completion?

I have heard it said that a leader's job is to keep peace in a company. I prefer to think of leadership as maintaining the harmony of various functions operating in mutual resonance to create an organization that performs like a symphony orchestra.

In fact, Ned Herrmann, who was head of management training at General Electric in the 1980s, predicted that, "The leaders of tomorrow will be maestros, not masters." [21]

The maestro need not have mastered every instrument in the orchestra. Instead, he assembles musicians with extraordinary skill on their particular instrument. His expertise is in leading them to a result that transcends what any single individual could accomplish.

The same thing can happen in a highly functional workplace. With balanced, servant leadership at the head, members of organizations, communities, families and nations resonate together, masterfully playing the same tune. The leader is simply the one who guides the tempo and the interpretation.

Learning as a Way of Life

Whenever I think of what it means to be a life-long learner, I think of my father. My mother once described him as "never bored or boring" because he was always learning something.

Most notably, his career followed the development of the electronics industry all the way from the crystal radios he experimented with as a boy in the early 1930s to the space shuttle program from which he retired in the late 1970s as a technical training instructor.

He remained curious till the end of his eighty-one years. As an instructor and a father he was a skilled leader in the manner of Lao Tzu. For in the end, his students and his daughter believed that we had succeeded on our own.

Leaders Must Continue Learning

As most of the attendees at the leadership academy I have mentioned aspired to become college presidents or VPs, each weekend session began with a talk by the president of the college where we were holding our workshops.

These presidents were astute leaders who were well-qualified to discuss the opportunities and pitfalls of rising to positions of greater authority and responsibility within any organization.

Several of them mentioned an unwritten (and therefore very powerful) assumption that when a person becomes a manager he or she should no longer need training. They explained that in some companies, a manager's admitting to wanting additional training can be tantamount to loss of credibility at best or loss of position at worst.

The problem may compound when a person ascends to the "C" level: CEO, CFO, COO, etc. The person at the top may be increasingly isolated from critical information or from subordinates who are unwilling to provide it—either out of fear of delivering bad news or because they assume the leader already knows everything about the situation.

So these wise college presidents advocated learning about leadership in every way possible, which included creating policies that encourage communication throughout the organization.

They were grateful to share their own experiences in career advancement. And they urged those who would be their successors to stay curious, humble and mutually supportive as leaders who love to learn.

Reflection 27

INTEGRATING DOING AND BEING

*Sooner or later, we reach a point of asking,
"Am I a human being or a human doing?"*

Where Is My Value?

We want to know: Am I worthy of respect because of who I am or because of what I do? Is my existence on this earth sufficient reason for me to be valued by myself and others, or must I accomplish some remarkable feat to earn validation for my being here?

To answer this question, we listen for guidance from our Wise Inner Counselor. Attentive to its presence, we find the moment-to-moment balance essential to a well-lived life.[22]

Being and Doing Are Both Necessary

Acting as a doer is not a bad thing. People who can get things done are essential in all walks of life. The Great Lights of all ages have been achievers. The essential element in all of our endeavors is who and how we are being in the process.

We do well to ask ourselves: As we move through our days, can we maintain a sense of wholeness and a kind self-regard? Can we include an element of spirituality in all of our doing? Can we stay in mindful touch with our inner reality?

When we are integrated with our True Self, we act from the heart. Our goal, then, is to let that center be our focus, the hub of our wheel, the motivation and the engine of our life and work.

Being and Doing Are the Twins of Life

One cannot exist without the other. They are two sides of the same coin, the daily expression of unity we take for granted because we are perpetually flipping that coin to see which side is calling for our attention.

What gets us into trouble in both our personal and professional lives is when we believe that being and doing are separate. If we believe that these functions are either/or propositions, we will be perpetually split between one or the other.

We inhabit a world of opposites: hot and cold, yang and yin, up and down, outside and inside. But we do not live in a world of absolutes. When you take a shower, the water is usually a combination of hot and cold. Being is never devoid of doing. And doing flows from the consciousness of being that motivates it.

Work Is Life and Life Is Work

Instead of focusing on opposites, what if we were to approach the activities of each day as a whole unit with various cycles of activity and rest that weave together throughout the twenty-four hours?

For example, consider this description of the Dalai Lama by Howard C. Cutler, M.D., who co-authored *The Art of Happiness* with His Holiness.

> His personal life was already so fully integrated with his work life that there was no separation between them...he didn't view any of his intensive activities in the world as work; these activities were simply an extension of himself as a human being.[23]

My impression of His Holiness is that he simultaneously extends his awareness inward for spiritual guidance and outward in service to others. He is like a living T'ai Chi who flows through each moment in a perfect integration of being and doing.

Life as Complementary Wholeness

We manifest what we believe to be true. If we are convinced that oneness is the highest truth of our beings, no matter who we are or where we come from, then unity is what we will perceive.

On a recent visit to Ireland I spent nearly two weeks in the company of individuals who exhibit the Celtic sense of oneness with the land and the seasons. They seem not to put much stock in separation.

During this trip I was fortunate to attend a private concert with the late composer Mícheál Ó Súilleabháin who was noted for his development of a unique approach to traditional Irish music. I had never heard the easy ornamentation of the *sean-nós*[24] vocal style played on a keyboard, and he captured it perfectly.

There was a fluidity to the sound that rippled like a perpetual stream from Mícheál's nimble fingers.

More amazing still was the clarity of the different voices that sang out from his left and right hands. I actually could hear separate tunes being played at the same time.

Each hand was playing a distinct melody that could have stood on its own. The performance brought the melodies together to create a third song of complementary wholeness.

A Uniquely Celtic Genius

When I had an opportunity to share with Mícheál what I had perceived in his performance, he agreed. "I'm for the median," he said.

We were practically finishing each other's sentences in the shared comprehension that his music flows from the crossroads where yang and yin, masculine and feminine, right and left brain hemispheres meet. The razor's edge that is the point of both unity and differentiation was the origination of Mícheál's compositions and the uniquely Celtic genius that he embodied. [25]

Expressing Perpetual Novelty

Not surprisingly, interviewers often described Mícheál as "hard to define." The man and his compositions truly comprised a genre all their own.

Because the *sean-nós* tradition on which much of his music was based is improvisational, there was a freshness in his performances that remains in his recordings.

He called his concerts "bespoke," meaning they were custom-designed. So every performance reflected his perspective at that moment. Both personally and professionally, he seemed always to be transcending himself.

Such perpetual novelty is also a characteristic of the Wise Inner Counselor. For me, listening to Mícheál play was to witness a demonstration of how I believe inner wisdom functions.

Bridging Worlds

Our True Self lives at the crossroads of being and doing. It lifts its gaze to commune with Spirit and then beholds us in our human state to guide us individually in all of our doing.

The Wise Inner Counselor is personal and unique to each of us. It is very concerned with the doings of our daily lives. It is also able to draw into our consciousness elements of universal truth that our human minds do not readily access.

It is this ability of our True Self to bridge worlds that makes it so effective. It sees beyond the limitations of time and space and yet is always engaged in the events of the present.

Here at the confluence of being and doing lies the secret of our greatest work.

Telling Ourselves the Truth

At its core, integrating being and doing means maintaining consistency between our thoughts, words and deeds. Are we being truthful about the quality of our inner dialogue? Surely, we cannot be truthful with others if we lie to ourselves.

When there is no conflict between what we believe and say and do, we are not at war with ourselves. When called upon to exercise integrity in the moment of choice, we are able to respond from a place of honesty and trustworthiness.

From the perspective of the Wise Inner Counselor, this is a goal to which we are daily urged to aspire.

Reflection 28

COMMITTING TO THE GREAT WORK ONLY YOU CAN DO

Love the life you are living and you will
undoubtedly live the life you love.

Detecting My Passion

When I was five years old I announced to my mother that I was going to be a famous actress. As a teenager I was convinced that my calling was on the stage.

Musical theater was my great love, and I pursued a career in entertainment with gusto. Yet things never quite clicked. The "big breaks" never materialized.

After several years of little progress and many disappointments, circumstances landed me in a series of executive support jobs where I began to notice that I tried to turn every position into one that involved writing. If I wasn't writing at work, I was composing epic-length letters to friends and family. Or reading books about authors and poets.

I finally realized that in my heart of hearts I was a lover of the written and spoken word. Nothing made me happier than the flow of inspired words that merged into poems or book chapters, articles or live presentations.

When I finally admitted that writing and speaking were the great work I came to fulfill, opportunities opened and living that passion did, indeed, become a way of life.

Only You Can Do It

Consider Jimmy Stewart's character, George Bailey, in the classic film *It's a Wonderful Life*. Like him, if you had not been born, the effects of your absence could have rippled across hundreds of lives—perhaps to their lasting detriment because you were not present to stem the tide of some calamity.

There is great work to be done in this world that only you can accomplish. Your unique contributions to the betterment of human-kind can only be made by you. In fact, I have read that there are individuals who can learn certain life lessons only from us personally, even if we never teach formally in a classroom.

Earth is often described as a schoolroom and, like the one-room school houses of by-gone days, it is up to the students to help one another along. The learning that comes from such interactions lifts everybody up and is one more way to discover hidden aspects of your purpose that emerge only in service of others.

Outpicturing the Ineffable

Your great work is a way of life. It is an essence and a tangible, felt sense. It is the spirit of you. The fragrance of you. Your great work is the ineffable quality of being that you naturally transmit every moment of your life. When you focus on what life presents to you, that special quality grows stronger every day.

Your Passion Is Already at Work

You do not really find your passion. It will likely find you. Then you notice it. Or detect it. If you look closely enough, you will probably observe it in the patterns of your best work.

What do you always do well? What gift or perspective can

you be depended upon to contribute to any situation? Let that be your focus in creating your great work.

You came into this life with a soul purpose and a passion to complete it. That purpose has a way of bubbling to the surface when you flavor your work with the zest of your True Self.

When you are fully engaged in the matter at hand, you cannot help but bring your special talents to bear on the situation. To give your best efforts to what is happening now is always your soul's essential purpose.

Believe in Your Purpose

Observe yourself. What type of work lights you up with an inner brilliance that is self-generating and perpetually self-renewing?

Infuse that essence into everything you do. Put your whole heart into your current occupation. Believe that the purpose you are seeking is also seeking you. Then let the great work that only you can do find you and embrace it with passion.

Life will thank you for it.

WHEN WORK BECOMES SACRED

Actualizing one's soul gifts can become a
· transcendent adventure that sanctifies both
the work and the one who performs it.

A Timely Example

As I was putting the finishing touches on this book, I happened to
have a conversation with my dear friend Brandon, who is an Irish
actor. I had recently watched his most recent film, which had finally
become available in the United States.

The story is an intense one that is set in rural Ireland in the
1840s. Brandon plays a man who loses everything. His crops fail, his
family dies, he is falsely accused of murder and must flee his home.
He has no livelihood and is surviving only through his skills as a
fisherman and herbalist.

For a time, he even loses his sense of self. His journey back to
his humanity through his gifts as a healer is a profoundly moving one
that unfolds against the rugged beauty of Connemara's landscape.

As we were discussing Brandon's powerful performance, he
told me how playing this role had changed him as a person. I could
easily imagine that it would, as watching the film deeply affected me
and those who viewed it with me.

Brandon said he had gained an understanding of the resilience of people like his character, who were still deeply connected to the land and knowledgeable in the ways of natural healing.

They were possessed of an inner strength that prevented them from giving up, even in the face of the most extreme privations. He said that living in that awareness for the month of shooting the film gave him a new perspective on his own life and work.

Then he told me something that I had noticed from how he had brought his character to life on the screen. There was a maturity of heart that shone through his performance—a quality that no director can bring out of an actor who does not already embody it.

When I mentioned this observation to Brandon, he said that he has discovered a sanctity in his calling as an actor which he had not recognized until he had to face the extreme physical and mental challenges of this particular role.

"I now understand and see the spirituality in the work," he said, and added that he intends to carry that quality with him from now on.

His statement thrilled me because that is exactly what *Doing Your Great Work* is all about. Fulfilling the work we were born for is to realize that purpose is sacred and uniquely elevating to our souls in an ongoing conversation between who we are and what we do.

Spiraling into Deeper Connection

When we bring the innate spirituality of our True Self to life, our determination to achieve a perfect effort elicits from us a stronger, more vital connection with that Self which unfolds like a spiral.

This deeper contact enhances the quality of all our endeavors as we further develop our natural gifts and talents. At the same time, we perceive our consciousness expanding in understanding the Wise Inner Counselor's guidance, which steadily leads us into increasingly refined states and stages of being.

Brandon agreed that this is what he has been going through.

And he is determined to retain the effect of this experience as a way of living and working in his chosen profession.

Achieving Our Greatest Work

Change is happening all around us. Yet Brandon's story illustrates how work performed with the passion of one's whole being will naturally reveal the Spirit that sparked it—as it has for generations.

When we follow the thread of a perfect effort, we step into the reality of our True Self. And all our endeavors are transformed into a labor of Love in action—the greatest work of any occupation.

A Bit of This and That

Notes

Acknowledgements

The Conversation Continues

The Purpose of Life

Notes

1. For more about multiple intelligences, see books by Howard Gardner. One of my favorites is *Changing Minds: The Art and Science of Changing Our Own and Other People's Minds* (Boston: Harvard Business School Publishings, 2006).

2. The original Total Professional model demonstrates twelve behaviors of top performers: **P**rompt, **R**esponsible, **O**rganized, **F**inancial, **E**xcellent, **S**avvy, **S**ocial, **I**ntegrated, **O**pen, **N**atural, **A**daptive, **L**eadership.

3. For a complete explanation of Soul Poetics, see Cheryl Lafferty Eckl, *Reflections on Being Your True Self in Any Situation* (Livingston, MT: Flying Crane Press, 2021). p. 76-85.

4. https://www.oliverlibby.com/videos/2019/2/26/future-of-work-and-entrepreneurship. See also: Bureau of Labor Statistics, https://www.bls.gov/ooh/construction-and-extraction/plumbers-pipefitters-and-steamfitters.htm (Accessed February 25, 2021).

5. Ralph Waldo Emerson, "Essay VII: Prudence" published in *Emerson: Essays and Lectures* (New York: Library Classics of the United States, 1983).

6. Stephen R. Covey, *The 7 Habits of Highly Effective People* (New York: Simon & Schuster, 1989).

7. "...for the support of this Declaration, with a firm reliance on the protection of divine Providence, we mutually pledge to each other our Lives, our Fortunes and our sacred Honor." The Declaration of Independence.

8. Captain Chesley (Sully) Sullenberger as interviewed by Katie Couric, CBS, February 10, 2009.

9. *When the Game Stands Tall*, Sony Pictures, 2014.

10. Learn more at www.JackCanfield.com.

11. John Welwood defines spiritual bypass as "the tendency in Western spiritual seekers to use spiritual ideas and practices to avoid dealing with their emotional unfinished business." See *Toward a Psychology of Awakening: Buddhism, Psychotherapy, and the Path of Personal and Spiritual Transformation* (Boston: Shambhala Publications, Inc., 2000) p. 11-21.

12. Maslow's Hierarchy of Human Needs:
    Survival Needs seek the necessities of life: air, water, food, sleep, shelter
    Safety Needs seek the security of protection, law, order, stability
    Belonging Needs seek affiliation with like-minded people or groups
    Esteem Needs seek self-worth through recognition of achievement
    Self-Actualization Needs seek fulfillment of personal potential
    Self-Transcendence Needs seek communion beyond the limits of self

13. For more about the internal shift that takes place within Esteem Needs and the importance of self-worth, see Eckl, *Reflections on Being Your True Self*, p. 107-115.

14. Adapted from Ned Herrmann and Ann Herrmann-Nehdi, *The Whole Brain Business Book, Second Edition: Unlocking the Power of Whole Brain Thinking in Organizations, Teams, and Individuals* (New York: McGraw-Hill, 2015).

15. Eckl, *Reflections on Being Your True Self*.

16. Eckl, *The LIGHT Process: Living on the Razor's Edge of Change* (Livingston, MT: Flying Crane Press, 2013, 2021) and *Thrive Through Chaos in Every Situation*. (See www.CherylEckl.com.)

17. Eckl, *The LIGHT Process*.

18. Eckl, *A Beautiful Death: Keeping the Promise of Love* (Livingston, MT: Flying Crane Press, 2010, 2015, 2018).

19. See Eleanor Roosevelt at https://www.goodreads.com/author/quotes.

20. Of a good leader, who talks little
    When his work is done, his aim fulfilled
    They will say, "We did this ourselves."
    - Lao Tzu, *Tao Te Ching* See https://www.goodreads.com/author/quotes.

21. Herrmann, *The Creative Brain*.

22. Eckl, *Reflections on Being Your True Self*.

23. His Holiness the Dalai Lama and Howard C. Cutler, M.D., *The Art of Happiness: A Handbook for Living* (New York: Penguin Books, 1998).

24. *Sean-nós* is a form of highly ornamented, improvisational traditional Irish singing that not only transports the solo singer and listeners to other worlds, it seems to descend from elsewhere with an innate intelligence that acts according to its own inner logic.

25. For Mícheál Ó Súilleabháin's biography and discography, see https://www.allmusic.com/artist/michael-osuilleabhain-mn0000468107. A film documentary of Ó Súilleabháin's life and work is also planned.

Acknowledgements

I Have Had a Lot of Help
There have been a number of instances in my life when I have felt that my soul had her own agenda and that I, in my outer awareness, just went along for the ride. I never could have predicted, or even imagined, that my future would unfold as miraculously as it has.

I have had a lot of help.

Life can be like that when we follow the promptings of our Wise Inner Counselor. Through the inevitable "thicks and thins" of a life lived with determination in the search for how inner guidance works, I have felt my soul being tutored so that one day I might realize that my True Self has been part of me every step of the way.

My heart overflows with gratitude for this extraordinary presence whose ineffable inspiration is the impetus and guidance for the insights I have offered through these reflections.

Special thanks to Brandon for sharing his story, and to the family of Mícheál Ó Súilleabháin for the opportunity to reflect upon meeting the maestro. Thanks also to Theresa McNicholas and James Bennett, and to my dear Stephen. Life is a miracle because we are in it together.

Finally, I would like to thank you, dear reader, for your kind attention as I have shared my thoughts on what a life well lived in the company of the Wise Inner Counselor can mean in the doing of your great work. This opportunity is a grace which I will always cherish.

The conversation of *Doing Your Great Work* continues with a companion book.

Have you ever longed for a friend who knows all your secrets and loves you anyway?

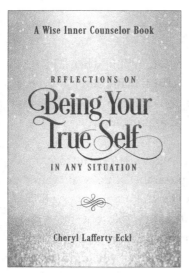

A Wise Inner Counselor Book

REFLECTIONS ON

Being Your True Self

IN ANY SITUATION

Cheryl Lafferty Eckl

Such a friend already exists within you as the powerful voice of inner guidance, known as your Wise Inner Counselor or True Self.

This inner guide holds you in deep affection and always tells you the truth because that is its nature.

Your Wise Inner Counselor knows you better than you know yourself and persistently urges you to be more genuine, more loving, more accomplished today than you were yesterday. It steadfastly points the way to your highest potential with faultless accuracy, and offers creative solutions that are uniquely applicable to you.

When you accept the unfailing guidance of this voice of limitless creativity, love and compassion, it will skillfully guide you through a world dizzied by the accelerating pace of ever-changing events.

Join award-winning author, poetess, life transitions facilitator and inspirational teacher Cheryl Lafferty Eckl as she shares her profound insights into the process of awakening your Wise Inner Counselor. Your life will never be the same.

164 pages * ISBN: 978-1-7367123-0-6

More from the Wise Inner Counselor™

Things are different now.
Normal has changed.

There is a tension in the air, a crackling of widespread disruption that threatens to overthrow our former ways of understanding who we are and what we do.

When chaos erupts, we lose our moorings. We are not who we were and we have not become who we will be in situations that are in constant motion.

Still, in the midst of changes on a scale we have never imagined, there is a way to do more than survive.

Now you can...
Thrive Through Chaos in Every Situation

This dynamic retreat experience engages your powerful inner guidance as you find meaning, peace of mind and a way to help others navigate the rough waters of life's most dramatic transitions.

Cheryl invites you to join her in:
- Transforming coping into processing
- Engaging your Wise Inner Counselor
- Transcending your former self
- Enhancing your creativity
- Improving your problem-solving ability
- Emerging as your True Self

See www.CherylEckl.com for details.

The Purpose of Life

The purpose of life is to be Love,
to embody its unity as unspeakable joy,
to flower in Earth's garden
as a hundred thousand blooms.

Imagine putting down roots,
drinking in pure air, reaching for the sun,
being washed by morning showers,
while basking in the great presence
that simply is the essence of being
that holds us all together.